Alan Stevenson

The ten Hymns of Synesius, Bishop of Cyrene

A.D. 410, in English Verse, and some Occasional Pieces

Alan Stevenson

The ten Hymns of Synesius, Bishop of Cyrene
A.D. 410, in English Verse, and some Occasional Pieces

ISBN/EAN: 9783744781947

Printed in Europe, USA, Canada, Australia, Japan

Cover: Foto ©Lupo / pixelio.de

More available books at **www.hansebooks.com**

The Ten Hymns of Synesius and other Verses.

The Ten Hymns of Synesius, Bishop of Cyrene

A.D. 410

IN ENGLISH VERSE

And some occasional Pieces

BY

ALAN STEVENSON, LL.B., F.R.S.E.

LATE ENGINEER TO THE BOARD OF NORTHERN LIGHTHOUSES

'Rouse thee, my soul, and drain thee from the dregs
Of vulgar thoughts; screw up the heighten'd pegs
Of thy sublime Theorbo[1] four notes high'r,
And high'r yet, that so the shrill-mouth'd quire
Of swift-wing'd seraphims may come and join,
And make the concert more than half divine.'

Emblems of Francis Quarles, 1644

[1] A large lute, for playing a thorough bass, used by the Italians — BAILEY.

PRINTED FOR PRIVATE CIRCULATION.

1865

EDINBURGH : T. CONSTABLE,
PRINTER TO THE QUEEN, AND TO THE UNIVERSITY.

PREFACE.

In early youth, I first came to know the name of *Synesius*, while reading the notes to that most interesting poem, *Idolatry*, by my much esteemed friend, the Rev. William Swan, who has therein paraphrased some lines from the Fourth Hymn of *Synesius*. In 1844 I sent to a clergyman some portions of the Hymns in English verse, which he thought fit for a place in a small volume, issued for the good of a church. It pleased God in 1852 to disable me, by a severe nervous affection, for my duties, as engineer to the Board of Northern Lighthouses; and I took to beguiling my great sufferings by trying to versify the whole *Ten Hymns of Synesius*. During many an hour, the employment helped to soothe my pains.

My great difficulties in dealing with the Hymns of Synesius, lay in steering clear of the leaning which the poet's early training had given to his mind to the mystifying thoughts of *Platonic Pantheism*, and also to his habitually employing the unintelligible phraseology of the *Valentinians*, which, however, I fully believe, he used with an orthodox heart. Such a

charitable view, it should seem by the notes of
Boissonade, in his edition of the Greek Poets, has
been expressed by Grabius in his Notes on Irenæus.
His words are, 'Hæreticâ voce, orthodoxâ autem
mente, de vero Deo, cecinit *Synesius;*' and elsewhere
he writes, 'Omnem fere Valentinianorum matæolo-
giam veræ theologiæ adaptavit Synesius, poeticâ
licentiâ abusus.' This subject has been admirably
treated, in a single paragraph of Leighton's *Third
Prælectio Theologica,* in which he cites *Synesius* himself as to the need of dealing most cautiously with
the mysterious doctrines of the attributes and per-
sonalities of the Godhead. It is as follows :—

' Et tamen balbuties mera est quicquid de illâ
primâ et increatâ felicitate et majestate loquimur ;
hic nos destituit non solum sermo, sed et cogitatio
omnis, ubi illum ἀνθείαστον, τὸν ὄντα[1] sine hominibus,
sine angelis, sine ullâ creaturâ, per infinita retro
secula in se solo monentem, et lucentem, et beatum,
et lætum contemplamur.

' Τίνος ὄμμα σοφὸν	Cujus oculus sapiens
Ταῖς σαῖς στεροπαῖς	tuis fulgoribus
Ἀνακοπτόμενον	præstrictus
Οὐ καταμύσει ;	non occludetur ?'

As a farther proof of the risk of dealing with subjects

---

[1] The late much esteemed Professor Scholefield, in his beau-
tiful edition of Leighton's *Prælectiones,* has a note as follows :—
' ἀνθείαστον quid sit, nescio ; num ἀνεξέταστον?' He then, on
the suggestion of a learned friend, adopts αὐτὸ ἕκαστον.

of this kind, so far beyond the teaching of Scripture.
I cannot avoid quoting an expression of desire for
pardon for any rashness of speech on this matter,
taken also from the Hymns of Synesius himself
(Hymn III. 153), immediately preceding that cited
by Leighton :—

> Μάκαρ ἵλαθί μοι
> Πάτερ ἵλαθί μοι
> Εἰ παρὰ κόσμον
> Εἰ παρὰ μοῖραν
> Τῶν σῶν ἔθιγον.

Synesius was an Egyptian, born at Pentapolis in
Libya, and dwelt chiefly at Cyrene.   By his first
training he was a Gentile, and was bred in a school
of Platonic philosophy.   About the year 400 A.D. he
was sent from Cyrene as ambassador to the Emperor
Arcadius Augustus, to whom he gave a golden crown
(as noticed in his Third Hymn) : and he, at the same
time, delivered an oration on the *Kingdom*, which
was esteemed as more dear than all gold.   About
410 A.D., when the citizens of Ptolemais asked of
Theophilus Alexandrinus that *Synesius* might be given
them as their bishop, that offer he himself refused,
and did not disguise the truth that, at that time, he
had not embraced the belief of the resurrection of
the body.   He, at the same time, confessed that, so
dear was his wife to him, that from her he was on no
account willing to be separated, and that, therefore,

he would not accept of the episcopal office, unless his wife and his religious scruples should be free from interference. To those stipulations *Theophilus* consented; and promoted him to the highest dignity of the priesthood, having respect, as Photius says, alike to the great probity of the man, and the well-known uprightness of his past life. In speaking of his style of writing, Photius commends it as 'sublime and grand, but inclining somewhat more to the *political*' (or rather probably *poetical*).[1] His letters, of which not fewer than 155 have been preserved, he also praises as 'flowing with grace and sweetness, and with strength and weight of thought.'[2] In those letters we trace his friendship with Hypatia, the famous mathematician and martyr, and the faithful follower of Athanasius in his Trinitarian orthodoxy.

Synesius wrote several works. Of those the most admired were his *Oration on Government*, his *Treatise on Dreams*, and his *Praise of Baldness*. He also gave an *Account* of the assault of the Barbarians on Pentapolis, and two *Books on the Providence of God*, and an *Account of his own Life*. Some think that his *Book on Dreams* was written while he was still a Gentile. He unquestionably extols the rites and oracles of the Chaldeans, and the mysteries and arts of the Egyp-

[1] Τὴν μὲν φράσιν ὑψηλὸς, καὶ ὄγκον ἔχων, ἀπολλίνων δὲ καὶ πρὸς τὸ πολιτικώτερον (or rather ποιητικώτερον).

[2] Χάριτος καὶ ἡδονῆς ἀποστάζουσι, μετὰ τῆς ἐν τοῖς νοήμασιν ἰσχύος καὶ πυκνότητος.

tians; and he undoubtedly embraces some of the opinions of both. In this view Dr. Cave does not agree; but thinks that *Synesius* had already become a Christian before he wrote his *Book on Dreams.* The fact that he not only, in a concealed way, wove the Chaldean oracles, as ribs, into the whole of that work, but even openly (αὐτολεξὶς) praised them, does not alter Dr. Cave's opinion. He concludes, indeed, by saying that no one can doubt that the Hymns of Synesius are the work of a Christian *Mystic;* and yet the *prow and poop* of those are derived from those Oracles. The same phrases and words, taken from those very Oracles, occur, Cave observes, in his *Hymns* and his *Treatise on Dreams.* Finally, Dr. Cave adds that *Synesius* obviously wished to transfer the *treasures* of the Chaldeans and the Egyptians to Christianity; as, in his little preface to that book, he seems himself to insinuate.

This naturally leads me to notice the opinions of the great Coleridge on this matter (as given in the first volume of his *Biographia Literaria*, 2d Edit. pp. 253-254), in a footnote on those words in the text, 'the ONE and ALL of *Parmenides* and *Plotinus* without *Spinozism.'* 'This,' he says in the Note, 'is happily effected in three lines by Synesius in his Third Hymn:—

'Ἐν καὶ πάντα = (taken by itself) is *Spinozism.*

Ἐν δ' ἀπάντων = a mere *Anima Mundi.*

Ἐν τε πρὸ πάντων = is *Mechanical Theism.*

' But unite all three, and the result is the Theism of
' St. Paul and Christianity.

'Synesius was censured for his doctrine of the
· Pre-existence of the soul ; but never, that I can find,
' arraigned or deemed heretical for his Pantheism,
· though neither Giordano Bruno nor Jacob Behmen
· ever avowed it more broadly.

> ' Μύστας δὲ νόος,
>   Τὰ τε καὶ τὰ λέγει,
>   Βυθὸν ἄρρητον
>   Ἀμφιχορεύων.
>   Σὺ τὸ τίκτον ἔφυς,
>   Σὺ τὸ τικτόμενον,
>   Σὺ τὸ φωτίζον,
>   Σὺ τὸ λαμπόμενον,
>   Σὺ τὸ φαινόμενον,
>   Σὺ τὸ κρυπτόμενον.
>   Ἰδίαις αὐγαῖς,
>   Ἓν καὶ πάντα,
>   Ἓν καθ' ἑαυτὸ,
>   Καὶ διὰ πάντων.[1]

' Pantheism is therefore not necessarily irreligious
· or heretical ; though it may be taught *atheistically*.
' Thus *Spinoza* would agree with *Synesius* in calling
' God Φύσις ἐν νοεροῖς, *the Nature in Intelligences;*
' but he could not subscribe to the preceding νοῦς καὶ
· νοερὸς, *i.e., Himself intelligence and intelligent.*

---

[1] Hymn III. line 187 (omitting φῶς κρυπτόμενον, added in
later editions).

' In this *biographical sketch of my literary life* I may
' be excused, if I mention here, that I had translated
' the eight Hymns of *Synesius* from the Greek into
' English Anacreontics before my fifteenth year.'

How deeply we must deplore that this translation
by ' *the marvellous-eyed one*' should never have been
published. I have made diligent inquiries as to its
fate ; but can learn nothing of it. I need not say
that I should not otherwise have ventured to try my
feeble and unskilful hand on the work.

One must wonder that *Synesius* should have escaped
the snares to which he must of necessity have been
exposed ; and when we consider the abominations of
blasphemy and impiety, into which Valentinus and
his followers (Basilides and others) sunk, we cannot
but think that the grace of God alone could have
rescued from perdition any one who had been trained
in such schools as those of the Platonists, and still
more that thereby alone should he have been enabled
to fill, with usefulness and credit, the office of pro-
minence in the Church, to which he was finally promoted.

It seems desirable, on account of the obscurity
which hides the subject, to add a few words as to
this arch-heretic, *Valentinus.* Being expelled from his
bishopric about the year 120 A.D., he seems to have
gone into voluntary exile to Cyprus, where he spent
a life of great impurity, and with his associates fell
into fearful blasphemy and advocated all iniquity.

He agreed with Basilides in holding the fabulous genealogies of Gods, and Æones of barbarous names, like those in Hesiod. He taught monstrous doctrines as to Christ's Incarnation, and also about various orders of beings, spiritual, animal, and fleshly. According to Tertullian, he wrote an *Evangelium*, and also a large Treatise on the *Origin of Evil*. In the Appendix I have given some extracts as to *Valentinianism* from some of the orthodox Fathers. I hope I have not, through inadvertence, circulated aught that is contrary to gospel teaching in my translation of the Hymns.

I think it right, as I have added no notes, to state that in the *Third* Hymn there will be found an allusion, at the foot of page 17, to *Epimetheus*, the brother of *Prometheus, Afterthought* and *Forethought*, ' which ·characteristics of the two brothers are recorded in ·various proverbs, *e.g.* τὸ μεταβουλεύεσθαι Ἐπιμη- ·θέως ἔργον, οὐ Προμηθέως—Luc. *Prom.* 7 ; Ἐπιμηθεῖ ·οὐκ ἔστι τὸ μέλειν, ἀλλὰ τὸ μεταμέλειν—*Synesius.*' —(See Liddell and Scott's *Lexicon.*)

The friends at whose request I have printed this feeble version of Synesius' Hymns for their pleasure, begged me to add a few small pieces of verse, which had accumulated in my own Scrap-book. They are chiefly translations, and a few reflections suggested by external objects, or by talk with friends. I trust they will be received with forbearance.

A. S.

May 13, 1865.

CONTENTS.

The Ten Hymns of Synesius.

Occasional Pieces.

APPENDIX.

Hymns of Synesius, Bishop of Cyrene.

A.D. 410.

I.

"Αγε μοι, λίγεια φόθμιξ,

COME, sweet-voiced lyre, to the soft Teian measure
And gentle Lesbian lays attuned for pleasure.
Breathe now, I pray, a solemn Dorian strain
To holy hymns : be there no notes profane.
I will not sing the praise of beauty's smile
That softly would young tender hearts beguile,
Nor tell of youths whose much-loved pleasing grace,
Breathes out in every gesture, and each pace.

The spotless Offspring of the Wise Supreme
Calls me to strike the lyre ; Himself the theme.
To tune for heavenly strains He bids to flee
The soft entanglement of earthly glee :
For what is strength, or what is beauty's crown,
Or what is golden store, or great renown,
Or kingly honour ? Is there one would dare
With thoughts of God or Heaven such dross compare ?

A

Let one his horse well guide, or bend the bow,
Or heap gold stores, with care unwearied slow ;
Let others pride themselves on glossy hair
That clusters o'er the snow-white neck so fair,
Or joy because a smooth and beauteous face,
'Midst boys and girls, bears off the palm for grace ;
But I would choose to lead a life serene,
Humble, by all, except my God, unseen—
A life most fit for youth, most fit for age,
In which wise poverty can calmly smile,
Untouch'd by all the bitter cares that rage
Round those who with the world their hearts engage.
Let me have but enough to keep me free
From suing beggary at my neighbour's door,
Lest hungry want should bend my soul to see
Nought but the loathsome cares that grind the poor.
List to the grasshopper, which sweetly sings,
Drinking the morning dew with flickering wings :
I too with humble and unconscious voice
And strings untaught by art would now rejoice,
For a mysterious, secret. heaven-born breath
Sweeps round me from above. around, beneath.
What strain at length will these strange throes bring
        forth !
He's the Beginning whence beginning came,
The One Unborn that far above the earth,
Enthroned on highest Heaven's stupendous frame.—
The Ruler and the Father of all things,—
In endless glory sits the King of kings.

O ! blessed Unity of Unities !
Thyself first Monad of the endless chain :
Who all things bountifully bringest forth
Super-substantially in ceaseless train ;
Whence Unity did seem at first to spring,
And was in Threefold power, diffused by way
Wondrous, with mighty powers of offspring crown'd,
Which from Thee well and beauteous round Thee
 play !
Rash harp be silent, nor profanely dare
The secret worship, which no rites declare,
To men to tell ; go, sing of things beneath :
Let Heaven be unpolluted by thy breath,
The soul alone may roam through worlds of thought.
(Whence by a holy origin 'tis brought
To dwell in man degraded on the earth.)
Yet uncorrupted and of heavenly birth,
This soul, entire and link'd unto its *Whole*,
Present in ever-changing forms itself presides,
Turning Heaven's concave, and does all control.
This heaven-born soul the starry courses guides ;
Part, too, by heavy bondage, down is bound,
To wed an earthly form upon this ground,
Disjoin'd from love parental, doom'd to drink
Misty forgetfulness and cares, that shrink
Before the sight bounded by joyless earth,
In wonder cheerless, seeks its heavenly birth.
Yet even in them the all-seeing God did dwell,
And light divine on blinded eyeballs fell ;

Yes, even in them who down to earth are hurl'd,
There springs a force their hearts that safely bears
Above the billows of this stormy world,
And upwards to their kingly home them steers.
O! blest, who shunning Nature's hungry cry,
Soars from this earth, with joyous spring on high;
Blest too! who, after death, and toils, and woes,
That gnaw on earth, enters Life's path, and goes
Straight to the Fountain fathomless, whence flow
Those unseen glories, which as yet none know;
'Tis hard for man to rise with outspread wings,
Borne upwards by the love of heav'nly things.
Do thou but nerve thy heart with the desire
Of godly wisdom's joy; to heaven aspire:
And soon thou 'lt see thy Father near thee stand,
And, bending o'er thee, stretch a helping hand.
For a soft ray from heaven will run to guide
And light thy way, and show that boundless land
Where intellectual lights for ever dwell,
And whence true beauty and true joy expand
From the deep fountains of God's love which well.
Upward, my soul! drink from th' Eternal Fount
Of heavenly good; with earnest prayer entreat
Thy Father! Halt not—leave this earthly mount,
For Godlike thou shalt be—in God complete.

KIRKSIDE, 1853.

II.

Πάλι φέγγος, πάλιν ἀὼς,

AFTER the gloom of night is pass'd away,
 Again we see the glorious, cheerful day ;
Again, my soul, with joyful morning songs,
Praise Him to whom all heartfelt praise belongs ;
He gives each day the cheerful morning light,
And circling stars that brightly dance by night.
The mighty mass of chaos boiling lay
In vapour wrapt, that floated dense and soft
Over the spiry fire, where the bright moon,
Cutting her lowest orbit, shoots aloft
Beyond eight whirling spheres that bear the stars,
A starless stream, in its vast billowy breast,
Ingulfing hurries counter-running streams ;
Ceaseless it moves, and knows nor pause nor rest,
Ever around the boundless mind, the King,
That shrouds the whole beneath His hoary wing.
A holy silence hides what lies beyond,
Where mind and thought unite in ceaseless bond,
One Fountain and one Root, whence all forth flow ;
Yet threefold splendours in His form we know :
From the great Father's bosom deep are found
The Son, who made the world, this image bright,
And the bless'd Spirit who on man has shed
His purifying, reconciling light.

One Fountain and one Root all blessings bear
That quintessential Germ whence life forth wells,
And th' inbred Light that clothes with splendours rare
Those blest abodes where pureness only dwells.
Thence the created but immortal choirs
Of angel chiefs, their sires benignant round,
Ever the praise of God and His First-born,
In choruses intelligent resound.
The angel host, rejuvenescent still.
Partly look backward to the beauteous birth ;
Partly behold the spheres intent and guide
Heaven's vault, and to the depths cast glories forth.
Yea, even where Nature brooding darkly bears
The rebel subtle crew, the demons named,
That giant race of strange, portentous forms.
By moaning winds which in the earth are framed, —
Of all Thou art the root ; all are Thy choice—
Past, present, and to come, of all the spring,
Whence all relations flow, silence and voice,
Nature of natures, all things Thou dost bring.
Father and mother, male and female, found
In Thee alike and Thee alone abound.
Ancient of Days ! Ruler, to Thee all hail !
(If with the voice we may Thy name make known,)
Root of the whole ! creation's centre, hail !
Monad of ceaseless numbers ; who alone
Didst form the angel-kings before unknown,
All hail ! all hail ! with Thee alone is joy !
Give ear in favour to my joyous lays !

Send wisdom's light and calm prosperity,
Not want nor worldly wealth's ensnaring ways
Drive away fell disease and loathsome lust,
And cares that gnaw the heart ; let not my wing,
Sin-laden, grovel on the earthy crust ;
But upwards with free pinions may I spring,
In untold raptures near Thy Son to sing.

III.

"Αγε μοι. ψύχα.

COME,'my soul, to sacred songs
    Give thy strength ; and calm to rest
Earth-born passions, and each power
Be to heav'nly thoughts address'd.
Stir up, my soul, the heavenly love
That burns within to God our King.
Offer th' unbloody Host with song
And full drink-offerings, as we sing.
O'er the wide sea, in distant isles,
Over the great and wide-spread land,
In cities and in rugged hills,
Where'er our feet securely stand,--
Maker of all, Thy name we 'll sound
In praise, through every land renown'd.
Upwards to Thee, O King, by night,
My soul oft soars, in tuneful flight ;
At the pale dawn, at burning noon,
And at sweet eve, my hymns I tune.

Bear witness, for you know it well,
Ye glittering stars, for you can tell,
And thou soft moon, whose gentle ray,
Yields to the brighter power of day,
Which rules o'er every lesser light,
And pious souls doth judge aright.
Lifting my weary wings, away
From the deep chaos to God's rest,
O! may I go, in cheerful day
To His fair courts and to His breast,
And, bending at His holy shrine,
Join in heaven's rites pure and divine.
Now to the sacred hills I go,
Upon those holy heights to pray,
And to bare Libya's deep defile
And southern verge I've wound my way.
Land! not polluted by the godless soul,
And where no worldly dreamers ever stray,
'Tis there the soul, from evil thoughts made whole,
From foul desires, from toils and woes set free,
And wrath and strife, which in the heart's core spring,
With holy tongue, O God, sings hymns to Thee.
O heaven, O earth, a reverent silence keep;
Stand still, O sea! breathe not, thou silent air,
And all ye winds be hush'd; ye curling waves,
Your angry tumults calm; and never dare,
Ye streams, to flow, nor fountains to well forth;
Let a deep silence rest o'er Nature's fields,
While pious tongues to the Lord's praise give birth.

Ye curling snakes! which earth polluted yields,
Be hid in earth. Go, idol-loving fiend,
Thou wingèd dragon, to the desert bare,
Nor cheer thou on the brood of hell-hounds dire,
To drown, with yells, each heaven-directed prayer.
O Father blest, drive far away the host
Of soul-deceiving fiends that fiercely tear
My trembling soul, corrupting all my deeds,
And scare my humble soul from earnest prayer.
O let our hearts be soothed by gentle care
Of holy messengers, who heavenward bear
To Thee our fervent hymns. I upward rise
Already to the goal of hallow'd rest,
Where sacred songs abide. The echo dread
Of God's voice thrills within my panting breast!
Forgive me, Father blessed, if too much
Of Thee I speak, or with unguarded touch
Thy throne approach. What eye can wisely gaze,
Or boldly try the holy Lord to see,
And yet not close, in guilty dread amaze,
Awed by the holiness they find in Thee!
Thy fires the shuddering gods of men dispel;
Their eyes from Thee cast down behold the earth;
Their quaking spirits dare not rise to dwell
Before Thee; but in awe they are cast forth
On what they cannot gain, and thus away
They, from Thy watch-tower, turn their darken'd eyes
To pierce the depths of light that boundless lies
Beneath. There is the seat of winds that play,

And bear the flowers of light that to Thee pay,
Offering back gifts which from Thee first came forth,
For to all things, O King, Thou gavest birth.
Father of fathers, all things, of Thyself,
Before Time, came, the Father ever One ;
The One before all Unities, Thou art,
Having no father, of Thyself the Son.
The Seed of beings, Centre of all things,
Eternal, unsubstantial Mind, whence springs
The Universe,—the Light that, e'er the day
Of things created came, eternal shone ;
The Fount of Wisdom true, the Mind deep hid
In its own brightness, e'er unchanged and One;
Parent and Life of ages, who dost rule
All minds and powers, the Maker of the whole,
Spirits and angels, nourishing all souls :
Eye of Thyself, Thou thunder dost control;
Fount of all founts, of all beginnings first,
O Root, whence every living root hath burst :
Unit of Unities, of Numbers all
The Source, the Mind that hast all ever known,
Both what has been, and what is yet to be :
One before all ; of all the Sum alone ;
Seed of all things ; the Root and highest Branch :
The Mind mysterious that canst all declare,
And leadest round the depths unspeakable
Thy circling orbits, through the boundless air :
Thou bringest forth, and Thou too forth art brought :
Th' eternal Father, to all eyes unknown.

Thy power appears, and Thou art often hid
In Thine own splendour; in Thyself alone
Thou wert in wonder seen, that Thou might'st bring
Thy Son, true Wisdom, Maker of each thing.
Thee Trinity, Thee Unity, I praise,
One and yet Three alike in all Thy ways ;
That severance our minds admit is still
The one and only Person of God's will.
Upon Thee, Son, by counsel wise shed forth,
(The Natural mind unspeakable,) none durst
Of Thee, first of all Natures, dare to say,
' From Thee a *Second* came, or *Third* from *First.'*
O Child unspeakable ! O sacred Birth !
Comprising what does bear, and what's brought forth !
A middle thing (not from *without* pour'd *in*)
Within the hidden plan which I revere
Deeply abides.   Th' unspeakable Father's will,
By wondrous birth, caused Thee to appear
In light and glory; with Thy Father still
Thou ever art,—His will and Thine the same.
Nor can time boundless the Son's birth proclaim,
The Father saw His Son, and He alone,
Nor oldest time can tell His birth unknown :
The pre-existent Son, to be reveal'd
With God the Father came.   O ! who will dare
In things unspoken and from man conceal'd,
Boldly and wickedly his thoughts declare ?
The blind man's words are blasphemous and bold.
O ! Thou who givest light to souls, withhold

From craft and crookedness the hearts of all
Thy saints, lest into hell's deep gloom they fall.
Father of Ages, and of those worlds bright,
Maker of gods, to praise Thy name is right ;
Thee souls intelligent e'er laud, O King !
Rulers of worlds, with sparkling eyes, e'er sing
Thy praise ; and souls in stars with joyful voice
In Thy bright glory, blessed Lord, rejoice ;
Round them, Thy person's glory ceaseless flows.
The whole assembly of the bless'd which rose
Throughout the universe, from pole to pole,
In boundless zones, and governing the whole,
Wise servants, faithful steersmen, who came forth
From the angelic host, by mystic birth,—
The noble race of heroes that, in ways
Conceal'd, wrought works of men now dead, Thee praise,
The soul upright, and what is apt to fall
Into the earth's dark mass adore Thy name ;
Thee, happy Nature and her offspring all,
Which Thou dost feed with genial winds, proclaim
Thy praise, O bless'd, who, from Thine endless store,
By Thy streams downwards, dost Thy bounty pour.
For Thou the Guide of worlds yet undefiled,
Nature of natures ! Thou wilt foster all
The race of man (of the eternal Type),
That thus the lowest mortal yet may fall
To share his portion of eternal life ;
Nor wrought God this, in justice but in love ;
Man's dregs to greatest hope he will exalt,

Nor what has lived to hell, will He remove;
It shall not die; but each shall have in time
His coming share of heavenly life sublime.
Of things that perish, the eternal band
To speak Thy praises ever do command—
To dance and sing.   Maternal mother fair,
In various works adorn'd and colours rare,
And all that live with different voices sing
With heartfelt joy, and common praises bring
To Thee sweet anthems that shall never end ;
Both day and night, lightnings that earth oft rend;
The sky and ether and the deeps of earth,
Snow, water, air, all bodies and all souls,
Seeds, fruits, plants, grasses, all things that spring forth.
Flocks, and all birds that fly between the poles,
Or crowds of fish that swim where ocean rolls.
Regard this soul, so pow'rless, weak, and spent,
In thine own Libya, in Thy sacred shrines,
On holy earnest prayers sincerely bent.
From me, in whom the clouds of flesh do dwell,
Thine eye, O God, can them at once dispel.
Then will my heart by hymns well nourish'd be,
Sharpen'd its thoughts by powers of fire divine ;
Grant that from flesh and sin I may be free,
Look down, O King, that light may ever shine.
But, while of forest life I bear the chains,
Blest God ! may gentle dealings soothe my pains,
And may no angry blast with baneful care,
Devouring life, from love of God make bare

My soul, and give woes that shall never rest ;
But by Thy gift, set free nor more opprest.
From holy meads, to Thee a crown I frame ;
Thy praises, Ruler of pure worlds, proclaim.
And to Thy Son, whose wisdom Thou brought'st forth
From Thy deep bosom vast by wondrous birth :
Though born of Thee, with Thee He dwelleth still,
That so His Spirit orders at His will
The depths of ancient ages, and the shores
Of the vast universe, even to the base
Of lowest beings ; and in boundless stores
Of glory, pious souls He will encase.
To all the cares and toils of wretched man
He looks, gives good, and sorrows all dispels,
Nor should we marvel that the God who made
The universe, black evils all expels.
King of the whole, I come a vow to pay
From Thrace ; for three years there compell'd to stay.
I dwelt beside the kingly palace hall,
Suffering sad toil and pains, that did appal
My heart, and on my back my mother-land
I bore ; the earth, with daily sweat of toil
Of wrestling limbs, and from my mourning eyes,
Through the long night, with tears my couch did soil !
But to all Temples, King, my steps me led,
That in Thy holy service I might toil ;
So bending, with wet eyelids there I lay,
So that my journey might not useless be.
Praying the angel ministers, whose sway

Was o'er Thrace's good land, and where the sea
Divides Chalcedon's fields, which they too rule—
Ministers holy, whom Thou, King, hast crown'd
And with angelic glory dost surround.
Help to my toils and prayers these bless'd ones gave :
But in my life I had no thought of joy,
For Thou my Fatherland had sorely grieved,
Thyself, O Ruler, free from all alloy
Of age.   While my soul faints and my limbs fail,
Thou grantest strength and cheer'st me, O my Lord,
From all my toils, and sweet rest dost me give,
And to all Africans Thou dost afford,
That for long times our hearts may ever know
The memory of Thy goodness and our woe.
To him who seeks, O give a holy life ;
Of labours, pains, and cares, O calm the strife
That gnaws the heart ; and to Thy servant grant
A thoughtful soul ; may worldly wealth not dare
To keep from God ; nor poverty that clings
Round our abodes, cast down my heart with care.
Whate'er to earth our soul draws down, whate'er
Forgetful makes of Thee, my Saviour dear,
O Father, wisdom's Fount, dispel with light,
From Thy breast make my intellect full bright ;
Comfort my heart by wisdom's beam from Thee,
And give Thy sign and token, for the way
That leads to Thee ; and from my life and prayers
The spirits of darkness ever drive away.
My body safe from all disease, O bring :

My spirit unpolluted keep, O King !
Now indeed Nature's murky stain I wear ;
And shameful lusts, earth's hated chains, I bear.
From disease, ills, and chains. O set me free,
My Saviour and Redeemer, for from Thee
Thy seed, a spark of heaven-born soul 1 bear,
Deep hid in man's corruption and in fear ;
For on the world my soul Thou placedst low ;
But in my soul Thou, King, my mind didst sow.
Thy child, O Blessed, pity; I from Thee
Came down to earth, a servant but to be :
But for a serf, a slave, now do I lie :
Nature, with magic arts, my heart does tie ;
Still in me dwell some hidden seeds and small
Of strength ; nor has it quenched my vigour all;
But many an upward billow o'er me bounds,
And when to God I look, my sight confounds.
O Father ! Thy child pity, who oft tries·
In upward thought, for Heaven ; but sad the sighs
That fleshly lusts oft bring to quench the light.
O King, send forth of heaven a cheering sight,
Send flame and fire that may sow the seed small
Within my brain.   O Father, place me all
In the power of the good life-giving Light,
Where Nature cannot thrust her hands, nor sight
Of earth shall be, nor the Fates' cords of woe
Backwards shall draw our souls that heavenwards go.
May treacherous men Thy servant leave and flee ;
Father, 'twixt me and earthly fights Fire be !

O Father, to Thy servant grant to spread
His wings of thought—may his soul suppliant dwell
Firm on the Father's seal, that mark of dread
For evil demons, who from earth's deep cell
Spring upwards, godless schemes in man t' expand :
But a sure watchword to those servants true
Who in the depths of the great world do stand,
Key-keepers of high flights to ether blue,
That they to him may open gates of light.
While on vain earth I creep, may I not cling
To earth'; but here give me the cheering sight
Of testing fruits, true words from heaven that 'spring,
And nourish in all souls the hope divine.
Over this earthly life I do repine.
Perish ye plagues of godless men, and might
Of towns, ye soothing snares that graceless smile,
Whereby the earth the soul deceived holds tight.
Its own goods it forgets, being so vile,
Until it fall into an envious share,
For cozening nature has two portions bare.
He who at table shows his hand to sue
The honey'd feast, his bitter share will rue ;
For weights oppose, and him will downwards pull,
And from two cups by earth's tyrannic rule
Pours out his life. Full pure and unalloy'd
Is God and all He gives. But if I'm cloy'd
With the sweet tempting bowl, I reach the shore
Of woe, and fall in snares, and feel the sore
That Epimetheus felt, and deep deplore.

But the uncertain laws I do abhor,
And to my Father's meadows free of care
Stretching my feet in flight I will aspire,
And shun the double gifts of nature's snare.
Giver of intellectual life and fire !
Behold me, and regard my soul that cries,
Which from the earth does upward flights desire,
Light up, O King, my heaven-seeking eyes.
Cut off all ties : and nimble make my wing ;
Chains of two lusts, by which false nature binds
Our souls to earth, unloose.   May I swift spring
Up to Thy halls and breast, where my soul finds
Its Fount.   To earth a heavenly drop I fell ;
Restore me, flying wanderer, to that well
Whence I was pour'd.   Grant me in first-born light
To be full mixed ; and that my Father's might
May keep me midst the holy choir, until
My share in heavenly hymns I may fulfil.
O Father ! grant that, in the light array'd,
No more into earth's vileness I may sink ;
But, while in forest life I am delay'd,
Let me, O Bless'd, of gentle fortune drink.

Dec. 27, 1864.

IV.

Σὲ μὲν ἀρχομένας,

THEE, at the break of sacred day,
    Thee, when the cheering daylight grows,
Thee, at the deepest noon so still,
Thee, when the fading daylight goes,
Thee, in the calm, majestic night,
Maker of all, I praise. And Thee,
Keeper of soul and all I see,
Source of true wisdom to the heart,
Before Thee deadly plagues must flee.
Thou only to the soul canst give,
From worldly cares which sorrow breed,
In heavenly calm on earth to live.
From such, O keep my bosom safe,
Thee, Hidden Root of all, to praise ;
Nor let rebellious sins that draw
From seeking Thee, my soul debase ;
Thee ! blessed universal King !
In hymns my soul desires to sing.
O Earth, and all thou hast, be still,
Ye creatures of the Father's will,
Form'd by His all-ordaining Word,
Let praises all and prayer be heard.
Let silent ether lift my song,
While birds are still, and rushing floods

Their babbling cease and breathless stand.
Ye whistling winds and roaring woods,
Ye hinderers of holy songs,
Demons in darksome dens who dwell,
And prowl round graves, avaunt !   My prayers
Shall scare you howling back to hell.
But ye. blest Ministers of good,
Obeying the Creator's will,
Who the remotest fields of space
And deeps unfathomable fill,
With gracious purposes draw near,
My hymns of joy and praise to hear ;
And upward, through the convex clear,
My prayers to God the Father bear.
O Unity of Unities,
Thee. Thought of Thoughts, I ever sing—
Father of fathers, only Spring
Of all beginnings, Thou bidst flow
All founts, and mak'st all roots to grow :
Thee only good—who world on world
And star on star through space hast hurl'd.
Fathomless Beauty, seed unknown,
Source whence the wings of Time have flown.
Father of spirits pure, that dwell
In spheres whose place no tongue can tell—
From Thee the Holy Ghost came forth
Like softening dew that floats o'er Earth:
New life is kindled in the dead,
And heavenly peace on earth is shed.

Blest God! by silence or by voice
I hymn Thy praises and rejoice,
By silence as by voice made known,
Is the heart's praise to Thee alone.
Thee, too, illustrious Son, Firstborn,
Primeval Light and Life of all,
I gladly praise with Him who came
From the dread Father at thy call,—
The Spirit who all wisdom knows,
Mediating source from whence all flows.
Thou didst bring forth the hidden Root,
By mystic union of all ties.
And thus the Father in the Son
On earths spread forth and in the skies!
The Boundless in a germ enclosed,
The God of Gods, the Son appear'd;
The Father all pervading fill'd
The Son who on this earth was rear'd.
Eternal One and Three Thou art :
Separate and united still.
What seems to us apart is join'd
By force of the Almighty will.
Yet still the Son springs forth and rules
His Father's kingdom in His might,
And gives what He receives to all
The glittering spheres.—His life and light.
The Father's mind unknown did bare
The Word, which with Him I do praise,
That Root, which from the First Root sprang,

Yet bears all else, Ancient is of Days ;
Thee One, the Source of all unknown,
Seen only to Thyself alone.
The source Himself did Thee beget :
Thou art in all ; by Thee alone
Nature, Heaven, Earth, and Hell are set
In their vast place, and taste the joys
Of passing life without alloys.
For Thee the starry vault does roll
Ceaseless, and young, and bright the whole ;
And at Thy word the concave vast
Totters, and in its course stands fast,
And the seven orbs in glory strung,
Are backwards in wild movement hung,
Because Thou bidst the myriad stars
Cheer the blind curtains of the sky,
And passing 'midst them, each his course
Unchanging seeks, beneath Thine eye.
Thrice blessed ! by Thy just commands,
Through the unfathomable waste
Of boundless space, the countless herds
Of worlds Thy bounty ever taste.
To all in heaven, hell, earth and air,
Thou giv'st of life and work a share.
Thou rul'st all minds, and sendest forth
All men and angels at Thy will ;
The dews of needful wisdom giv'st ;
Each one hath his befitting fill.
Souls, Lord ! Thou giv'st to those whose life

And energy are link'd with sense ;
To the blind race of those who hang
On Thee alone, Thou dost dispense
From out Thy breast, beauteous and vast,
The power by which their races last.
Thou art unseen ; from Thee forth flow
The streams, that earth to cheer come down ;
Viewless eternal wisdom's light
That comes all else with grace to crown,
Are sun-shone on the universe.
Source of all light, from which flows light,
That came and went, lightener of eyes,
Dividing day from ancient night.
Type of all mind, the Son is He,
Whose gifts are to His creatures free.
Father unknown, transcending thought,
Unspeakable, no tongue can sing
Thee, Mind of minds, Thee, Soul of souls,
Thee, Source whence natures all must spring.
Behold Thy servant kneels on earth !
In blindness, pity, Lord, and send
Light to my soul ; from pain and care
That gnaw my life, Lord me defend.
O bid the fiend of hell depart,
The demon of the Flesh, whose snares
Hang round my body, heart and soul,
My words, my deeds, my thoughts, my prayers.
O bid them leave me, make them flee
Who give their strength to earthly love,

Who hinder those who seek the Lord,
And scare us from the heaven above.
A holy angel mighty send
To be my guardian and my guide—
In heaven-taught prayer to keep my soul,
And body in temptation's tide ;
Let not disease my body try,
And let not sin my spirit stain,
Oh, from my memory ever blot
All fleshly lusts and longings vain.
Even through this earthly life may I
In holy praises soar on high ;
So when the chains that bind to earth
Are snapt, I stainless shall spring forth,
Up to my palace-home—Thy breast,
The fountain of my life and rest.
Stretch forth Thy hand, draw me, and call
My suppliant soul from nature's thrall.

V.

Ὑμνῶμεν κοῦρον νύμφας,

LET us celebrate the Son
        Whom the Virgin spouse brought forth;
From the Father's counsels deep
Sprang the seed that gave Him birth.
He in human flesh appear'd
Offspring dread, of Virgin born—
He to souls in darkness came

Harbinger of coming morn.
Wondrous Child that knew'st the Root
Whence revolving ages spring.
With Thy Father, Light of lights,
Nature's darkness scattering,
Framer of the solid earth
And the countless orbs so bright,
Saviour of men, whose hearts receive
Thy sanctifying, cheering Light.
Thy word Sol's chariot obeys,
The fountain of unquenchèd light,
The Moon her heifer-face displays,
For Thee to chase the shades of night :
The fruits are born ; the flocks are fed
For Thee; Thy wondrous power calls forth
Genial life-giving light and heat
Which fatten all the roots of earth.
From Thy bosom budding forth,
Came light and intellect and soul.
Pity Thy child, prison'd in flesh,
And bound by Fate's harsh, blind control,
My vig'rous limbs from maiming sores,
O keep.   Persuasiveness be mine ;
And good my deeds, that so renown
From Sparta and Cyrene shine
Upon my soul.   Not sorely prest
By woe, right peaceful may I live,
Fostering good, and may my eyes
See Thy bless'd Light that life does give ;

Thus, purged from Nature, may I run
My heavenward course, and may I shrink
From earthly cares, but panting, long
Of the Soul's Fountain deep to drink.
A holy life grant me, who sing
Thy Root, O Father, to make known,
Coming from Father and from Son,
And sitting in Thy blessed Rest,
Sing His praise, and to be blest,
For from this God came forth my soul.
Hail! Father's form! fount of the Son!
Son's seat, the Father's image whole,
Son's power. Hail! Father ever bright!
Pure Spirit, centre of the Son
And of the Father, Three in One,
Send me that cheering heavenly light
That sprinkles the parch'd soul's dull wings
Ere into perfect bliss it springs.

VI.

Μετὰ παγᾶς ἁγίας αὐτολοχεύτου,

FROM out the holy self-engender'd Spring,
   Th' unutterable Unities above,
Immortal God's illustrious Son we'll sing,
Only-begotten of His Father's love;
And with the flowers of wisdom's hymns we'll praise
His Name, and honour Him with holy lays.
Him the great Father's will, by wondrous birth,

Forth from His bosom fathomless brought forth,
That thus His hidden love our God might show
To souls that wallow'd in the earth's dark slough.
The Father's wisdom and His glory came,
And still shed forth flow from that endless spring;
And Thou, His sole begotten, Thou the frame,
The germ and secret of each new-born thing.
O great Original of all the worlds,
From intellectual essence Thou couldst call
Forms hid from man, but in Thy counsels traced
Before all time, good, beauteous, wondrous all.
The heavenly spheres in wisdom guidest Thou,
Thou, as a flock, feedest the countless stars
With light and heat; Thou rul'st th' angelic host,
And bind'st the demons fierce in during bars.
Thou also, dwelling with poor mortal flesh,
Sendest Thine undivided Sprite on earth,
Men to deliver from the doom of death—
Thy gift returning whence it issued forth.
Propitious, hear Thy praise; vouchsafe to me
A quiet life; nor let Euripus roar,
Nor his fierce billows, nor the blast that moans
Amidst the woods, disturb my spirit more.
Keep me from ills of body and of soul,
And stay the hurtful impulse of desire;
The snares of poverty and wealth restrain;
To holy deeds may my meek soul aspire;
O crown me with a mild, persuasive voice,
So may my spirit peace and quiet find;

Nor toss with care, but still in hope rejoice
In the fruits of a chasten'd heavenly mind.

VII.

Πρῶτος νόμον εὑρόμαν

JESUS of Solyma ! God's Son !
   Son of Virgin ! bless'd of fame !
I first taught this lyre, in measures
Lately tuned, to praise Thy name.
Gracious King ! O grant Thy favour
To my notes ; accept the song,
While we praise the Son Immortal,
Wondrous God, of Godhead sprung ;
God the Father who unfolded
Endless ages, as they run ;
God the Son, the world's Creator,
God and man conjoin'd in One.
Thou art God, of boundless wisdom ;
Heavenly angels know their Head,
Wondrous too, for in death's darkness,
Thou wert buried with the dead.
Through a mortal womb Thou camest
Down to earth from heaven afar ;
Doubt and wonder filled the Magi,
When they saw Thy rising Star.
Their wisdom fail'd ; their art, they find,
Brings no solution to their mind.
' Who 's this Child, to us now born ?'

Awe-struck, trembling, thus they sing.
' In Him see the Godhead hidden.
' A God-man and a heavenly King,
' Thou art God ! let incense rise
' With grateful odours to the skies.
' Kingly art thou, and we bear
' Purest gold and spices rare.
' Thou art born of mortal womb.
' Myrrh is fitting for the tomb.
' These, O Lord, to Thee we bring.
' God, mortal man and heavenly King.
Thou the earth of sin didst purge,
Didst quell the angry ocean's surge.
From the liquid fields of air
Dravest the demons of despair,
And from the lone and darksome grave
The soul of sinful man wilt save.
O God, from heaven who didst descend,
And death's and hell's dark portal past.
Th' enclosures of the grave didst rend.
And broughtest life to man at last.
O heavenly King ! incline thine ear.
The praises of Thy saints to hear !

VIII.

'Υπὸ Δώριον ἁρμογὰν

BLEST Immortal! born of Virgin,
     I would celebrate Thy reign,
On the sweet-toned ivory lyre,
Tuned to solemn Dorian strain.
Keep my soul, O King of Glory,
From all sin and changes free,
Day and night in each temptation
Let my strength be found in Thee.
May my soul and heart drink deeply
From the spring of sacred truth ;
May strong limbs and glorious doings
Be the gifts that crown my youth.
May my life in blessed calmness,
Flow straight on to latest age,
Blest with health and crown'd in honour,
With the wisdom of a sage.
My brother keep, whom, lately passing
Through the portal of the tomb,
Thou hast call'd to dwell for ever
With Thee in the heavenly home.
Past are all the cares and sorrows,
Tears and heart-corroding cares,
Thou hast quench'd the flame of anguish,
Gracious hearer of my prayers !

My loved sister and her children !
In their home may they abide
Quietly.   Oh, 'neath the cover
Of Thy wings them safely hide.
And my dearest wife, the partner
Of my best, my purest joy,
Keep from sickness and from trouble,
In true love, without alloy.
One in heart and one in purpose,
May our wishes never stray
From the pure and holy bondage
Seal'd upon our wedding-day.
Let us deem this union holy,
And preserve it true and pure,
Mindful of the purer friendship,
In the heavens, that shall endure.
When our souls throw off the bondage
Of this earthly life below,
May we rise from worldly troubles,
And from sin's eternal woe,
With the blessed saints and angels,
Ever songs of praise to sing,
Of the Father, God Eternal,
And Thy might, O heavenly King !
Thee at length I'll sing in heaven,
With purer songs and higher lays—
And on harp soft and harmonious
Sound the Saviour's worthier praise.

IX.

Πολυήρατε χύδιμε,

THEE, Desired of all the nations,
     Glorious and immortal King.
Virgin born, of Solyma,
Thee my feeble tongue would sing.
From the bright and golden gardens
God had planted, Thou couldst chase
That fell serpent, old Deceiver,
Of the wicked earth-sprung race.
Down from heaven to earth, a stranger,
Man with man, Thou cam'st to dwell ;
Through the grave, death's gloomy portal.
Thou divedest to lowest Hell !
Thousand hosts of souls imprison'd
In the chains of death stood round :
Ancient Hell was chill'd with horror,
Backward shrunk the hungry hound.
From the souls of saints that loved Thee,
At Thy word, their chains straight fell ;
And that holy legion, glory
Gave to God in deepest hell.
Countless throngs of airy demons
Quail'd before the ascending King ;
In their courses, pale with wonder.
Stood the stars nor dared to sing :

But the smiling fields of ether,
Where harmonious fountains spring,
With a mystic sevenfold chorus
Welcome back the heavenly King ;
Day's harbinger and Hesperus soft
Are full of holy, chasten'd mirth ;
The Moon, with hornèd crown, fresh tipt
With streaming light, the stars leads forth :
The Sun, out of his mellow'd light,
Golden paths before the King
Weaves, for he knows Thee, God's own Son,
Of his own light the cause and spring.
Thou on wings mountedst far above
The outmost bounds of ether blue,
There to rule over countless orbs
All-fill'd with beings wise and true—
Orbs that swiftly float and smoothly,
Through a region full of light,
In the silent sphere of heaven,
Where God's gifts are pure and bright.
There, nor time, untired, deep-flowing,
Nor hungry plagues that howl for prey,
In the deep and billowy forests,
Earth-born worms shall sweep away.
But the eternal flowing season,
Never young and never old,
For blest souls, enduring mansions
Evermore shall still unfold.

X.

Μνώεο Χριστὲ,

CHRIST ! Thou Son of God that reignest
    In the sky, remember me—
Me, Thy servant, helpless sinner,
    Who those hymns have sung to Thee ;
Free, oh ! free me from the bondage
    Of the lusts that dwell within,
Springing up as weeds envenom'd
    In my soul, debas'd by sin.
Jesus ! Saviour ! make me see Thee,
    In Thy splendour and Thy light ;
Soul and body then shall know Thee,
    The Physician's healing might ;
God the Father—God the Son,
    Great and glorious, we adore ;
God the Holy Ghost, life-giver,—
    God Triune for evermore.

KIRKSIDE. *Oct.* 13, 1855.

Occasional Pieces

SUGGESTED BY EXTERNAL SCENERY,
BY VARIOUS WRITERS, AND
BY FRIENDLY TALK.

A Thought at Capel Curig, North Wales.

HERE Nature frowns in her majestic ire—
 High tow'ring cliffs and precipices dire :
Yet do they seem to point to Wisdom's path ;
Upturn'd, they look as if the Almighty's wrath
To pray had taught the rugged rocks ; that we,
When they are forced to bend, His wrath may flee.
 July 17, 1829.

Evening Reflections.

WHENCE comes this sadness o'er the soul,
 This deep, reflective, sombre mood,
That chains us with unfelt control
 To muse at evening's hour, and brood
Sadly on all that late was gay,
 As if for us there ne'er could be
An orient morn,—a sparkling day,
 Like what has pass'd so joyously ?

Why do we sigh, watching the light
 That leaves the mountain-tops at eve ?
Why list the beetle's drony flight,
 As if we there had aught to grieve ?

Why turns the tearful eye to pierce
   The gloom that shrouds the lonely vale.
As if the heavens a portent fierce
   Sent on the rude breath of the gale

Say, is it not foul guilt that taints
   With gloom the spirit's inward peace
Which else each scene of nature paints
   In holy, God-like soothing grace !
The world is hid that we may hear
   A small, still voice that melts the soul
To tender, holy, saintly fear—
   To heavenly peace and self-control.

Ah ! wayward man ! thy careworn heart
   By wild remorse now fiercely riven,
Feels as a deadly, venom'd dart,
   This hour of calm thy God has given :
But did eternal peace illume
   Thy soul, a rapture pure and calm
The heart would now possess—the gloom
   Of Night would be grief's surest balm.

Liverpool, *July* 14, 1829.

The Dream.

UPON a lone and distant sea-girt tower,
　　Round which the ocean dash'd its crested foam,
I mounted guard at midnight's dreary hour,
　　(I was a stripling then—but late from home) :
I gazed with rueful look upon the wave,
　　And shiver'd at the shrill sad wintry blast.
No voice was heard ; all was still as the grave :
　　Between each gust, I held my breath, chain'd fast
By a chill torpor, nor my wonted round I pass'd.

Forth look'd I on that wild and lurid sky :
　　Reckless the clouds career'd o'er its expanse :
The loud wind whistled ; the shrill sea-bird's cry
　　Distressful came.　I watch'd the flitting dance
Of those who their unholy vigils keep,
　　Night-gazers, robed in sapphire's icy hue ;
They revel when the dewy flowers do weep,
　　Rending with fiendish laugh the welkin blue,
Dwelling in ether's fields, a wild unhallow'd crew.

Scarce had they wov'n their dance's mazy round,
　　When on the wild waves they a bark descried :
After long wanderings, she was homeward bound,
　　Few souls she bore, for they had hopeless died.

There was a maiden whose long-pining heart
  Delusive hopes had wither'd ; but her soul
Was cheer'd when o'er the water the light bark
  Was gaily bounding. She forgot her dole,
  And the past griefs that poison'd her life's bitter
    bowl.

My young heart bled.   I saw the maiden wave
  The kerchief which some faithful swain had given.
When parting from her native strand !   How brave
  The bark did bound to seek her holy haven !
But the enchanters fell of yon dark sky
  Had mark'd the prize, and led them to their fate ;
Watching their course with askant, evil eye,
  And in their hellish purposes elate,
  Each joy'd in their foul plot with rapture to his mate.

Onward she sped upon the fatal reef ;
  I waved, to guide her from the beacon tower,
Yet onward still they sped.   O God ! what grief
  To mark the triumph of unhallow'd power !
They sank ; I heard the deadly shriek of woe,
  Like the last trumpet's clear and thrilling note :
And as they found their icy graves below,
  The evil curses of glazed eyes smote
  My heart, and chill it, even now by night, I wot.

I gazed into that troubled, angry wave,
  That swell'd with pride at this its triumph won,

Methought each tenant of the coral grave
  Hail'd my lost soul in hell, ' Undone ! undone !'
But soon I saw a white arm on the sea,
  Waving that kerchief ; and the pallid face
Of the lone maiden faintly smiled on me,
  With love's forgiving look and holy grace.
  She sank ! I saw no more that sweet angelic face.

    BELL ROCK LIGHTHOUSE,
     March 16, 1830.

Hymn.

IN every shifting scene of life,
  In peaceful joy, midst war's wild strife,
    My God, I trust in Thee ;
To Thee at noonday's burning hour,
To Thee, when wintry tempests lower,
    With confidence I flee.

When midst the horrid gloom of night,
My soul is chill'd with guilty fright,
    And driv'n to dark despair,
Humbly I turn my hope above,
And sing Thy mercy and Thy love
    In holy pious air.

Thy pardon of my sin I seek,
My weakness and my woes I speak,

Embolden'd by Thy grace ;
Though blotted now by sin's foul stain.
Refined by salutary pain,
 I yet shall see Thy face.

Not on my works I rest my claim
(Though holiness be still my aim),
 But in the sacrifice
That Jesus offer'd on the tree,
Forgiveness, Lord, I ask of Thee,
 For every form of vice.

Yet penitence shall wing my heart,
My soul from sin I 'll strive to part :
 And daily to adorn.
My life with some new grace I 'll try.
The pride of life and lust of eye,
 To view with holy scorn.

Though, like the lily's spotless leaf
No penitence, no holy grief,
 My soul can e'er make pure.
Yet shall the Saviour, in His love,
By intercession made above,
 Favour for me secure.

Triumphant songs, immortal lays.
Eternal notes of boundless praise

To Christ, their Priest and King :
To God the Father, God the Son,
And God the Spirit, threefold One,
    The saints in Heaven shall sing.

KINTYRE, *Augt.* 29, 1830.

A Vision.

A GOLDEN palace in the skies
    Draws from the earth my worldly eyes :
And holy trains of angels seen
Dress'd in bright robes of glory's sheen—
A fair enamell'd ample mead
Before its front in verdure spread,
And through it flows a crystal brook
Whence stooping each the waters took.
Meanwhile sweet sounds of music came,
Praising the high Eternal Name,
Forth from the Temple's holy gate,
(Whence came the bright angelic host)
And wonder-struck, they all did wait
As if in holy rapture lost.
And censers waved they up and down.
And scatter'd fleecy vapours round,
Which rising wreath'd a holy crown,
That the sweet Saviour's temples bound :
Then did they join the holy song,
And the immortal note prolong ;

And each one beckon'd with his hand,
And bid me join their glorious band.
To Thee, my God, I praise will give,
Who thus dost make Thy servants live
Eternally in joys serene,
Midst golden dome and meadows green,
And bidst them crystal waters drink
From brooks of sweet and soothing sound,
And eat life-giving fruits from trees
That bloom the year eternal round.
Then may I all the lusts deny
That tempt on earth the fleshly eye :
And though a life of pain I spend
On earth, yet at the world's dread end,
My Saviour's sacrifice I'll plead
(Who for lost sinners once did bleed
On the accursèd Cross's tree),
In wondrous love to rescue me.

Who would, when glory is the prize,
In those bright mansions of the skies,
Thus reckless of such hopes still live,
For all this passing life can give !
The proudest heart this world contains
Has woes and cares, shames and annoys ;
Then, who would pause to count earth's gains,
And barter them for heavenly joys ?
Flee from the charmer, for her song
Will captivate thy heart ere long :

Arise and don thy pilgrim's weeds,
Address thyself to holy deeds ;
Let night in earnest prayer be past,
Thy days in prayer and holy fast ;
Thy body let the servant be
Of what alone God wills in thee.
Each thought, each wish, each hope be
      given
To praise thy God and rise to Heaven ;
Each power be consecrated then
To serve God and do good to men.
Only for sins let tears be shed ;
Only that hungry souls be fed,
Thy tongue should give its hallow'd sound,
And this its chiefest use be found.
Thine earnest prayer and upturn'd eye
Be ever pointed to the sky,
And all thy hopes, and all thy sighs,
Be for thy sins, and to the skies !

KINTYRE, *August* 29, 1830.

O Salutaris Hostia,

O HOLY Victim giving life,
      And opening Heaven's gate of light,
When dangers press and hostile strife,
      O grant us aid, O give us might.

To the one Threefold Deity,
    Be everlasting glory given,
Who hast prepared eternity
    Of life for all the saints in Heaven.

June 20. 1830.

Lines.

THAT lark now confined to his prison of sorrow,
    Looks ruefully round on the closely-wired cell ;
No hopes of sweet freedom to cheer him to-morrow,
    With roaming through greenwoods or deep woody
      dell.
But when Night round his prison has cast her grey
    covering,
    In his sleep he oft dreams of the forest so gay,
Now over a bank of sweet primroses hovering,
    Or heavenward springing to meet the young day.

So when thoughtful and lonely at evening reclining,
    Or toss'd on the bed of long sickness and pain,
At the sorrows of life we are deeply repining,
    Thy goodness, O Father of Love, we arraign.
But when Night round our aching hearts gently is
    closing
    Those curtains of slumber that bring visions bright,
Then Faith, on Thy Mercy, O Father, reposing,
    Fills the bosom with hope and the heart with delight.

EDINBURGH, *Nov.* 7, 1830.

Veni Creator Spiritus,

COME, Holy Spirit, in Thy might,
    And send from Heaven Thy hallow'd light,
        To bless us with its ray ;
O Friend of all who are in need,
From whom all perfect gifts proceed,
        Light of our hearts and way !

Thou who our sorrows canst console,
Belovèd Inmate of the soul,
        The heart's refreshment dear ;
In labour Thou our only rest,
Our shade when with noon's heat opprest,
        Thou dry'st the mourner's tears.

Most blessed Light, most holy Fire,
The inmost hearts do Thou inspire
        Of all the faithful here ;
For here without Thy holy Name,
In guilty man is nought but blame,
        Nought in his heart but fear.

O wash our souls from sin's foul stain,
Refresh our barren hearts with rain,
        And heal our wounds, we pray ;
Our pride and stiffness do Thou tame,
Our coldness warm by love's pure flame,
        And guide us in Thy way.

To all Thy faithful, Father, give
(Who in Thy trust and worship live)
The seven gifts divine ;
Grant us in holiness to wait
The opening of the heavenly gate,
And taste of joys sublime.

January 18, 1831.

Easter Sunday.

Victimæ Paschali Laudes.

TO the pure Paschal Victim raise
Your sacrifice of fervent praise !
Christ is the Lamb that by His death
Redeem'd us from the curse and wrath :
And to the Father reconciled
Sinners from life and heaven exiled.

O think how wondrous was the strife
Between conflicting Death and Life,
When Christ the Lord of life did die,
And reign immortal in the sky.
Say what thou sawest in the way,
Mary ! at break of that blest day.

' I saw the grave where Christ was laid,
The sheet in which He was array'd.
The living Lord Himself I saw,
And Him adored with holy awe ;

While, straight before my wond'ring eyes,
He rose in glory to the skies.

' The Angels' voices record bear,
   " The Lord is risen ; He is not here ;
He goes before to Galilee ;
There you again your Hope shall see." '
O Christ ! we know that from the tomb
Thou truly didst in glory come.

Alleluia ! let us sing
The glories of the Victor King,
Who tasted Death and every woe
That man is heir to here below !
Thou, Christ ! wilt pity and forgive
And ever make Thy chosen live.

   January 18, 1831.

Approach of Cholera.

THE angry pest is passing by ;
  And now, in every street,
Chilly disease, corruption rank,
  And loathsome death we meet ;
He will not spare the sceptred prince,
  Nor mitred priest regard,
He 'll crush them in his ruthless rage
  With grasp right chill and hard.

He will not spare the peasant bold,
  Nor pass the cottage by ;
To men he brings a warning dread ;
  He summons all to die.
He speaks God's wrath and curse to men,
  And checks man's towering pride,
That dares to challenge Heaven's decrees,
  And God's own laws deride.

We thought our intellect sublime,
  In its portentous march ;
And o'er our giddy heads we raised
  Freedom's triumphal arch ;
We boldly burst the sacred ties
  Which erst our fathers bound ;
And monarch's rule and churchman's sway,
  Our people have disown'd.

The hoary sire the pest won't spare,
  In his paternal grace ;
Nor yet the saint-like beauty of
  The mother's anxious face ;
The tender puling child shall feel,
  The racking tortures tear
Life's feeble cords, and, fainting, pass,
  To Heaven's ethereal air.

The manly form of youth shall fall
  Before his noisome breath,
His godlike head and eagle eye
  For ever sunk in death.
The blighting chilly vapours, too,
  Shall blanch the maiden's cheek ;
And glassy stillness shall o'er-spread
  Those eyes which mildness speak.

'Tis late to weep—'tis late to pray,
  In this sad night of woe ;
The fell pest passes fiercely by,
  He beckons you to go.
No time in kind farewells now waste :
  For in the last embrace,
The lip is chill'd ; and livid hues
  O'er-spread the once loved face.

The saving blood of Christ alone
  In that dread night can cheer,

When the ruthless pest walks gloomily,
    And scatters wide his fear ;
Saint-like the Christian, then, alone,
    Amidst those mortal throes,
Shall in the Saviour's blood expect
    The end of all his woes.

EDINBURGH, *Jan.* 26, 1832.

On my dearest Mother.

OF gentle soul, to all that knew her dear,
    The tender mother, best of friends lies here,
Whose darling wish was comfort to impart,
To cheer the drooping, soothe the aching heart.
Love, truth, and meekness breathed in all she said ;
Faith bless'd her life, hope smooth'd her dying bed.

Dearest of mothers ! best of friends, farewell :
These words sincere a son's affection tell :
Through life thy virtues were his joy and pride,
In death his best example and his guide.
Our social hopes and fears, alas ! are o'er ;
A mother's love now cheers our hearth no more.

    March 1846.

Anicii Manlii Torquati, Severini, Boethii,

De Consolatione Philosophiæ,

(A.D. 455.)

Liber Primus, Metrum VII.

> Nubibus atris
> Condita nullum
> Fundere possunt
> Sidera lumen.

THE stars, by pitchy clouds obscured,
. ' To mortal eyes no light afford ;
The sea itself in summer seen,
Glassy, pellucid, and serene,
When angry winter tempests urge,
Boils up a foaming muddy surge ;
The headlong flood that ploughs with pride
The lofty mountain's rugged side,
By fragments which itself hath rent,
From the rude rocks, is oft up-pent ;
If thou wouldst see Truth's image bright,
And walk in wisdom's ways aright,
Bid vain deluding joys avaunt ;
Nor let pale Fear thy pillow haunt ;
Put Hope's deceitful dreams to flight,
And Grief, fell tyrant of the night ;
Darkness obscures the fetter'd soul,
That sinks beneath their dark control.

OBAN, 1833.

Boethii de Consolatione Philosophiæ,

Liber ii., Metrum i.

Hæc cum superba verterit vices dextra,

L IKE Euripus' tide,
    That foams in pride,
Is Fortune's cold suspicious hand :
We change our fate at her command,
    Dreaded kings are crush'd
    Low in the dust ;
The vanquish'd oft is raised on high,
To smile on false prosperity.
Sighs or groans will fortune hear ?
Will she lend her dull cold ear
To sorrow's tale, or wipe her falling tear !
    No—no—she loves to laugh
    At wretched men who quaff
    The bitter cup she gives ;
    In every hour man lives.
She shows a wonder to his sight,
And mocking coldly tries his might
By reckless changes every hour,
Lifts up or casts down with fell power !

OBAN, 1833.

Boethii de Consolatione Philosophiæ,

Liber II., Metrum IV.

Quisquis volet perennem
. Cautus ponere sedem,

WOULDST thou thy cot secure,
Place where it may endure
Age after age ;
Spite the rude tempest's breath,
And ocean, threat'ning death,
In his proud rage ?
Seek' not the cliff's dire brink,
Nor thirsty sands that drink
The briny tide.
The sweeping tempest's might
Beats on the mountain's height
With angry pride ;
And the false sands, though fair,
Thy mansion will not bear
Above the sea ;
Seek some low sturdy rock,
Where neither ocean's shock
Nor wild winds be ;
Though hungry waves devour
The buildings of man's power,
Thou 'lt pass thine age
Secure in that calm nook ;
Nor needest ever brook
The tempest's rage.

OBAN, 1833.

Manuela, the Spanish Mountain-Maid.

BEFORE me now, in simple grace,
    The Spanish mountain-maid I see,
Who, o'er her native Pyrenees,
    Trode many a weary step with me.
Fearless, in childlike innocence,
    O'er lonesome heath, through silent glade,
She was my guide, for two long days,
    That merry Spanish mountain-maid !
The dark mantilla cast its shade
    Upon her face, which well might be
A model for the sculptor's art,
    So perfect was its symmetry.
The ample brow and hazel eyes
    So full of tenderness and glee,
Her dimpled cheek and rosy mouth,
    Were clothed in virgin modesty.
She told me all her simple cares,
    And all her girlish hopes and fears ;
She had no guile ; nor did she think
    The world could blame her smiles or fears.
Her brother, and *one* still more dear,
    Had gone to serve their rightful King ;
And oft she ask'd me, if I thought
    They would return before the spring :
For they had fix'd the bridal day ;
    And Manuela's gentle heart

Beat high with hope ; she seldom thought
 Of war's rude shock that might them part.
No doubt could dash her ardent hopes ;
 She had a pure confiding soul ;
Short were her fears ; and down her cheek
 But *one* bright tear of sorrow stole.
Well may King Charles his standard plant
 On Spain's fair soil, if every maid,
Like Manuela, sends her swain,
 For right and law to draw his blade !
Well may he hope, if Spanish maids
 Maintain his crown and lend the might
Of sweet persuasive lips, bright eyes,
 And loyal hearts t' uphold his right !

Los Passages, near San Sebastian,
 August 1834.

St. Ambrose's ' Deus Creator Omnium.'

From Augustine's Confessions.

O GOD ! who mad'st the wondrous whole,
And ever guid'st the whirling pole,
Who cloth'st the day with golden light,
And giv'st Thy grace of sleep to night :
Grant that our wearied limbs, by rest,
To useful toils be more address'd ;
That sleep our burden'd minds may free ;
And all our cares be heal'd by Thee.

EDINBURGH, *Jan.* 9, 1835.

To Elizabeth.

L ADY ! on thy brow appears
 No wrinkle of fast fleeting years :
No grief from sympathy that flies
Has blanch'd thy cheek or dimm'd thine eyes :
Thy spirit yet is young and free,
And joys in childlike purity.

O ! would to Heaven my prayer could bring
The eternity of such a spring,
Where budding hope alone appears,
The harbinger of happy years,
Where all the past is pure and true ;
No carking care of sickly hue
Dares, with a doubt the future blight,
Full of gay dreams and visions bright.
Yet, gazing on thy marble brow,
Albeit all unruffled now,
Thy deep blue eyes serenely gay,
And on thy coral lips' soft play,
Or on thy cheeks' soft mantling flush,
Where conscious beauty seems to blush ;
O maiden ! who can fail to feel
Thy heart is not a heart of steel,
But form'd for every kind emotion,
Friendship sweet and pure devotion ?

Full well I ween, at evening hour,
The gentle time for magic's power,
That oft a trembling nameless feeling,
Through all thy gentle bosom stealing,
Speaks of a blank hope ne'er supplies,
And all thy guesses still defies ;
Till love shall draw the veil aside,
That shrouds from view a fairy bride.

Start not, nor deem that thoughts so new,
So unsuspected and untrue,
May not be conjured but by spell,
Of nodding bush and dropping well :
There is a magic slow, whose will
Owns a fair empire wider still,
Of all that's good and great creative.
And of its idol imitative ;
Of weal or woe alike, its power
May work a change, in one short hour.

Then deem not, lady, when the voice
Of gentle whispers shall rejoice,
That th' inner heart, which thou dost veil,
When hopes exult or fears assail,
Deem not the gloomy midnight shrine,
Where incense burns and tapers shine,
Can chase away the gentle sprite,
Or quench love's pure undying light ;

And, therefore, lady, thus I pray,
Thy heart so gentle and so gay,
In love may never know the chill
Of cherish'd hope, requited ill.
The bitterest of those earthly woes
The true confiding soul oft knows ;
But, from my inner heart, I bless
Thee whom ev'n angels would caress :
For thou art surely of that mould
Of earth's fair daughters, born of old,
Whom ev'n the angels wont to cherish,
With love that could not change or perish.
Lady, to thee I dare not show
How much of grief this heart shall know,
When, toss'd upon the boundless sea,
With longings, that shall turn to thee.

1834.

Morning.

Imitated from the Spanish of Melendez.

UP from thy nest, O bird of morning,
    Thy merry carol singing,
To welcome in the new-born day,
    That in the east is springing !
See where the dappled rosy flush,
    And saffron beam of morning,
Bursts from the clouds, with hallow'd light,
    The mountain-peaks adorning.
The gentle breeze now stirs the clouds ;
    They pass away, disclosing
The purpled western wave, where late
    Aurora was reposing.
Up mounts the sun ; herb, leaf, and flower,
    That yester-eve were pining,
Refresh'd display their silken folds,
    With glittering dew-drops shining.
All Nature the returning sun,
    Source of light, life, and motion,
Beholds with heartfelt calm delight,
    And hails with mute devotion ;
A thousand perfumes from the flowers,
    Like incense rise before him ;
The choristers of boundless groves
    With untaught hymns adore him.

O 'tis an hour of tranquil joy,
    Just when the day-light 's breaking,
To feel a stirring gentle hope
    Within the bosom waking.
We gaze on Nature's wide extent,
    The valley and the mountain,
List to the whispers of the wind,
    The warblings of the fountain.
We let the eye in quiet rest
    Upon the lake that 's sleeping,
Unruffled by the passing breeze,
    And in bright sunshine steeping ;
We pry into the darksome grove,
    Where sunlight cannot enter,
A still sequester'd favourite nook,
    Of peace the very centre ;
We tread the bright elastic grass,
    With starry flowers enamell'd ;
Or scale the rugged craggy cliff,
    By fear and care untrammell'd ;
We drink the crystal brook and breathe
    Pure air that floats around us ;
Thoughtful we dive far into space,
    Beyond the skies that bound us.

These are the calm and pure delights,
    By Nature's bounty given,
That, stirring through our mortal frame,
    Turn Earth itself to Heaven.

An undefined and boundless joy,
    In every breast awaking,
Kindles soft fancies in the soul,
    When, the deep silence breaking.
Each living thing bursts forth in songs
    Of gratitude and gladness ;
And o'er wide earth there is no trace
    Or memory of sadness.
Then meet me, maiden, at the dawn,
    In haste thy couch forsaking,
From brightest visions of the night,
    To brighter truth awaking ;
Beneath the shade of yonder beach,
    Where first our love was plighted :
Oh ! meet me, lady, with the love
    Distrust has never blighted.

July 28. 1836.

To the ' Ringing Stone' at Balaphetrish, Tyree.

MYSTERIOUS Stone! rude, shapeless as thou art,
    Thou seem'st unconscious of the ocean's rage.
Or winter-tempests that for many an age
Have howl'd around thee ; say, hast thou a heart
Deep prison'd in thy mass, that feels the smart
Of others' woes—woes of the gentler kind,
Which spring up easily in woman's mind !
For, touch'd by maiden's hand, with gentle art,
Thou givest sighs, that tremble on the breeze,
Which sweeps around the western Hebrides,
Such as Andromeda, from ocean's cave,
Might breathe responsive to some sorrowing maid
Whom slighted vows or dear hopes long delay'd.
Have driven to seek, near thee, a lonely ocean-grave.

HYNISH, *May* 13, 1842.

Lines at Evening.

FAST the purple light is fading
      From the far untroubled west ;
And swift night, the dull earth shading,
      Weary man invites to rest.
Glittering stars begin to twinkle
      In the clear, cold, eastern sky,
In that sea, without a wrinkle,
      Bright their imaged glories lie.
Deep within the cold blue waters,
      To the musing eye it seems,
Midst those stars, that ocean's daughters
      Sporting, catch their fleeting gleams.
Trusting to that sight illusive,
      If we tempt those waters still,
Quick will fade the dream delusive,
      Blasted by their ruthless chill.

Thus, through life, we 're onward going,
      Toss'd by youth's vain hopes and fears,
Flowers and thorns alternate strewing,
      Slaves of woman's smiles or tears ;
But, at length, the golden season
      Of our youthful dreams fleets past,
And the cold, clear voice of reason
      Speaks, our hopes and joys to blast.

To Three Sisters.

Chilly age at length comes mourning
Over joys that did but seem;
And tell us (sad and solemn warning!)
All our life has been a dream.

January 1843.

To Three Sisters.

G̎RACES from far Cambria's shore,
   Sisters three of Mona's Isle!
Every motion of your lips
   Is prophetic of a smile.
Countless[1] is the changeful mirth
That illumes your household hearth.

Margaret![2] pearl-like emblem, thou
   Of a calm, kind, constant heart;
Catharina's[3] spotless soul
   From her soft eyes seems to start:
Dora![4] gift from heaven sent down,
Latest gem of beauty's crown!

January 29, 1843.

---

[1] ἀνήριθμον γέλασμα.—Æsch. *Prom. Vinct.* 90.
[2] *Margarita,* a pearl.
[3] καθαρός, *pure.*
[4] Δῶρον Θεοῦ, *gift of God.*

Inscription for Llynon Woods.

GENTLY, ye gales of heaven, oh gently fan
    Dear Llynon's graceful ash-trees' feathery shade ;
Gone are the days when Howel Dda to man
    Gave laws that spared the misletoe and laid
The gentle ash-tree low.[1]   Here oft has roam'd a
        maid
    That loved the soothing shelter of those trees,
That cast no gloom, but kindly oft detain
    At noon some faithful pair, or temper sun and
        breeze
To one with toil foredone —a sleeping swain.
    Like them is she, ever by kindness known ;
The troubled spirit in her look may read
    A woman's worth, her kindness in the tone
Of that soft, soothing voice.   Be then agreed,
Ye winds, to spare those trees, a gentle maiden's
        meed.

April 2, 1844.

---

[1] Those laws valued the misletoe ninety times higher than
the ash.

To M.

MY fancy straight begets whate'er my heart desires ;
   And as we ramble ceaseless on our way,
In every change of scene, mine eye admires
   Thy floating form. Green alley, mountain grey,
A copse's tangled covert, gardens trim,
   Or roadside hut, with well whose gushing sound
To passing ear is mute,—all these my fancy's whim
   Have link'd to thee. With thee I pace the round
Of yonder garden walk ; that mountain's side
   We climb together ; through the coppice green
Or hedge-row elms, thy fairy step descried,
   'Startles their gloom ;' mine eye, a limner's, keen.
Some form bent o'er that well with pitcher, spies,
And straight her upward look shows thy soft sunny
   eyes.

MAIL COACH, LANGHOLM WOODS,
    May 7, 1844.

To M.

THROUGH this bare silent vale, 'midst hills, we
 speed ;
 Yet can mine eye spy out, beneath some rock,
A tranquil home, from sun and tempest freed,
 Whence the lone shepherd eyes his scatter'd flock.
A scene like this recalls those words of thine,
 Which with a gentle 'proving tone to me,
Yestreen, thou spakest of thine age and mine.
 I would that on that moss-grown stone, by thee,
I now were placed ! Sweet maiden ! I could show
 That little thou dost know how, in my heart,
Dearly I prize the mellow, tranquil glow
 Of kind affection, that thy looks impart,
When those, who in the *gloaming's* light rejoice,
 Seek, for their *stay*, thy mild and kind assenting
 voice.

SHAP FELL., *May* 7, 1844.

The Goat of Mona's Isle.

BENEATH an ash-tree's cool and friendly shade,
   Browses a bearded goat, on Mona's shore;
But soon his upward look welcomes a maid,
   Whose fathers on their shield his image bore
In days long past, when Druids ruled the land.
   Look on her gentle form; Oh! hear her voice
Of kindness as she feeds, with friendly hand,
   Her aged favourite.   Mark her and rejoice.
For oft, of old, Irminsul's mystic shield,
   Struck by a maiden's hand, sounded the note of
     death.
Where now, by very gentleness conceal'd,
   Burns, in that maiden's heart, a holy faith
That is by graceful kindly deeds made known
To watchful eye alone—to the rude world ne'er shown.

LONDON, *May* 12, 1844.

Lines at Midnight.

Air—'SELMA.'

WITHOUT, the wintry wind
    Moans sadly through the woods;
The voice of many waters roars,
    From deep, hoarse murmuring floods.

We bend before Thy throne,
    O Lord! at this dread hour;
We fear not, Lord, for we can trust
    Alike Thy love and power.

Lord! for Thy Son's dear sake,
    Our darkness change to light;
And from all perils us defend,
    And dangers of this night.[1]

December 10, 1844.

[1] Second Collect at Evening Prayer.

Lines, during a Winter Sunday Walk.

Air—' BALERMA.'

NOISELESS we pace the leafless woods
   That skirt the frozen lake ;
Good Lord of love and grace ! may we
   From them a lesson take !

Those trees again will bud before
   The soft warm breath of spring ;
The swallow in that crystal flood
   Again will dip his wing.

How slow are we, Lord, to believe
   That Thy good Spirit's breath
Can wake our wintry hearts to life.
   From sin's cold, loathsome death.

Blood-sprinkled at Thy Cross we 'd stand,
   Though once we did despise,
Jesus ! Thy meek and lowly name,
   Now precious in our eyes.

For guilty, trembling worms like us,
   Sweet words the Saviour spoke ;
Our proud and frozen breasts were thaw'd,
   And heart-sprung tears awoke.

'The smoking flax I will not quench,
  Nor break the bruisèd reed ;'
Blest Saviour ! how Thou know'st our woes,
  And send'st the grace we need !

In every woe we still behold
  Thy mercy and Thy care,
Which send the winter's chilling blasts
  The summer to prepare.

Dear Saviour ! may we give Thee all ;
  Nor fear to own Thy name,
Before a scoffing world that tries
  To put our Hope to shame.

How sweet, with those we love on earth,
  To pace the wintry wood !
And tell, with hearts of common joy,
  Dear Lord ! that Thou art good !

O turn, once more, dear gentle friend,
  While tears bedew thine eyes ;
And mark that redbreast's confidence,
  That wakes a kind surprise.

All summer he disdains to seek
  Our window's shelter'd nook ;
But when the wintry tempest moans,
  He loves man's friendly look.

Winter Sunday Walk.

In this, the Saviour seems to speak ;
  And calls us to our home,
By all the griefs of this cold world,
  O'er which we thoughtless roam.

Taught by His Spirit, we shall feel
  That all our woes are light ;
After a dark and stormy day,
  He sends a calm, clear night.

O may He touch our hearts with love !
  Grateful each morn we'll rise ;
Each night lie down in humble hope,
  To meet Him in the skies !

BRIDGE OF EARN, *Dec.* 10, 1844.

To Margaret.

DEAR gentle wife, this Christmas morn,
  Waking to taste of heaven's bliss
Vouchsafed to man when Christ was born,
  I greet you with a kiss.

And with that kiss I breathe a prayer,
  That as we tread the thorny way,
At Heaven's gate we still may rest,
  Each joyful Christmas day.

Oh! mark the cheerful hearth that lights
  Yon casement, through the flaky drift:
So sparkles 'midst the year this day,
  The blessed Saviour's gift.

O Lord! still as Thy birth comes round,
  More hallow'd may our union be,
Seal'd by Thy common faith and bless'd
  By common love to Thee.

Christmas, 1844.

Christmas Sonnet.

DEAR Misletoe! dread emblem once of rites
    Gloomy and cruel, that of yore began
Beneath the spreading oak, the Druids mystic year.
    I hail thee now, a sign of peace to man.
Green bough of truce, budding in winter's night,
    Thou dost remind us of our coming Lord,
Who as a gentle child, in great humility,
    Came down to bless us with His saving Word.
Come let us hail this day with awful joy,
    Soon as light dawns, long sought for, in the east.
Far be from us the Pagan's gloomy rites,
    And Romish arts that shame the Christian Feast.
Come to the pure, clean table that the Lord hath
    spread.
Here in the wilderness, where He our fathers fed.

December 25, 1844.

Christmas Sonnet.

COME, welcome Christmas day, dear Christians
   all !
   To-day our blessed Lord from heaven came.
To visit us poor sinful worms on earth :
   Let us rejoice with fear, and praise the Lord's
      dread name.
Oh ! early to His temple let us go,
   His name to praise and for His grace to pray.
Welcome this day of love, this morn of joy,
   Dear followers of the Lord—this is His natal day.
Keep ye this festival apart from the rude world,
   Yet not austerely, lest ye seem to slight
God's wondrous love—permitting bigot zeal
   To cloud the glories offered to your sight.
And when day's past, welcome the peaceful night,
For night must usher in the eternal heavenly light.

   Christmas, 1844.

To M. S. S., with a Misletoe Bough.

LADY ! the dark green wintry bough,
    Deck'd with a streak of gold,
And glistering drops, snow-white,
That wreath'd the marble, gloomy brow
    Of the Druidess of old;
    Lady ! that misletoe to thee
(When thou no thought couldst have of me)
    I sent at dawn of light.

Wherefore, oh maid of Mona's Isle,
    At early dawn of light,
    Sent I that bough to thee ?
Was it that thou mightst, with a smile,
    Wreathe, with the berries white,
    Of that mysterious bough,
Thy raven hair and placid brow ?
    L'an-neuf-an-gui ! [1]

No, Margaret, to my musing ear,
    The leaves of sober green,
    Fringed with the golden streak
Of gentle worth and soul sincere,

---

[1] The Druid's call at the first day of the year; it means, ' New year with misletoe.'

Brighten'd by mirth serene
(As stars in polar seas are seen),
    Most eloquently speak.

But, Lady Margaret, need I say,
    That, spotless, icy, cold,
Those glistering berries to my heart,
    A double sense unfold ?
For, while of thy pure, pearly [1] name,
    The emblem true appears ;
Their coldness bids me think thou scorn'st
    Alike my hopes and fears !

January 1, 1844.

[1] *Margaret* means a *pearl.*

Jehovah-Jireh.

GENESIS XXII. 14.

WHAT wondrous faith does Abram show
   A stranger in the land ;
To raise an altar to the Lord,
   He halts at God's command !
Nor does he shrink, but lifts the knife
To take his only son's dear life.

A father's heart was bleeding there :
   The darksome wood he trode
In silent woe ; while Isaac bore
   The self-consuming load !
Yet saw he, in his offspring dear,
The type of Him who should appear.

In him the aged patriarch sees
   The Child whom God has given :
The parent of a promised seed,
   Countless as stars in heaven :
Still, faith and fear forbid to chide.
His God—' Jehovah will provide.'

Bound on the altar, Isaac lies !
   The knife is raised on high :

F

But God from heaven commands to stay
   His hand ; and to his eye
Offers, within the thicket caught,
A substitute, with mercy fraught !

So JESUS, nail'd upon the cross,
   To save our souls did die,
And by His perfect holiness,
   The law to satisfy.
How then can we His love neglect,
Or His great mercy dare reject ?

AT SEA, 1846.

To R. A. M. S.,

On his birthday. Edinburgh, 25th March 1852 (written in
his Bible and Prayer-book).

READ in this blessed Book, my gentle boy;
    Learn that thy heart is utterly defiled.
That JESUS, Love Incarnate, died (great joy!)
    And sinners to JEHOVAH reconciled.
This day five years thou numberest; and I
    Write on a bed of anguish. O my son,
Seek thy Creator, in thine early youth;
    Value thy soul above the world, and shun
The sinner's way; oh! seek the way of truth.
    Oft have we knelt together, gentle boy,
And pray'd the Holy Ghost to give us power
    To see God reconciled, through Christ, with joy:
Nought else, but Christ brings peace in sorrow's
    hour.
O may pure Bible truth, I ever pray,
Guide heavenward all thy steps through error's mazy
    way.

EDINBURGH, *March* 25, 1852.

' Benefactions,'[1] sent to Martha L.

THIS cup that so gorgeous appears
    With its rosy festoons and its gold,
' That seems, by the air that it wears'
    Of a Persian or Tyrian mould :
This cup—to a kind friend I owe :
    ' She gave it, and gave me, beside' •
A saucer that matches it so,
    And a plate that I place by its side.

This ' Portion'[2] we take ere we rest,
    And again at the dawn of the day ;
It tells us of joys pure and blest,
    And whispers from heaven, ' Come away.'
And this little volume that shows
    All the snares of ' Declension'[3] that lie
In the Christian's path, as he goes
    To his bright home far off in the sky.

And Leighton—that teacher of love,
    Of hope, faith, and patience, and prayer,

[1] See Cowper's verses under that name.
[2] Hawker's *Poor Man's Morning and Evening Portion.*
Winslow on Declension.

Who calls us to glory above,
    From earth's wilderness gloomy and bare ;
And many sweet ' Messengers' too
    That flit, day by day, 'cross our sight,
Tracts, that speak, through this dark night below,
    Of heaven and its mansions of light.

All these, and sweet books for our babe,
    And warm fleecy coats for his chest,
And many things, such as in verse,
    By my poor pen can ne'er be exprest ;
All these to our kind friends we owe,
    And we owe them a large debt beside
Of kind wishes, kind thoughts, and kind prayers,
    Which we ne'er can repay though we 've tried.

How swift is the course of the star,
    That upward shoots into the sky !
How fleet are the lightnings that far
    In night's gloom 'cross the blue vault oft fly !
But fleeter and swifter our prayer,
    As it mounts to our Father above ;
And rich are the blessings we share,
    When we ask for each other in love.

1848.

On the Comparative Influence of bare and rich
   Scenery on the Mind of the Inhabitants of a
   Country.

J OYS deep-drawn and mysterious do they taste—
   The mariner, who ploughs the pathless plain
Of desert ocean, and the lonely swain
Who guides his flock across the treeless waste !
For upward through the fields of starry light,
Their souls unconscious shoot, and ether vast.
Seeking, beyond the fall, the cherish'd past,
Dimly remember'd 'midst the soul's dull night :
They to man's ancient home and kindred high,
Upwards from cheerless earth are often call'd ;
No hindrance have they to the upturn'd eye
Of holy hope ; their hearts are unenthrall'd
By the soft joys which bright earth gives to those
Who on her bounteous lap 'midst groves and lawns
      repose.

KIRKSIDE, *August* 26, 1853.

On the Rugged Patches in Starry Nebulæ, seen through powerful Telescopes.

THEY who with telescopic gaze can thread
  Wide ether, orbs do find countless and vast
   and bright,
That shed through space a mild diffusive light ;
Yet here and there rents, ragged, black and dread,
In that soft haze of silvery light appear.
' What are they ?' oft my longing soul inquires,
' The ancient seats of long-extinguish'd fires ?
Or are they gateways to those regions drear
In which the unreclaim'd, cast forth, do fall
Through outer darkness, cheerless, without end,
Hastening away from God, and Heaven, and all
That we should love !' Our hard hearts to amend,
Forth from that sky's rent vail, sad whispers come,
That make us breathless pause amid earth's busy hum.

KIRKSIDE, *September* 12. 1853.

On Memory as an Agent of Retributive Justice.

HOW indestructible is Thought ! The ridge
    Of lofty Cordillera, yea, the globe
Itself, like smoke, shall pass into the womb
Of nothing, whence they came. The sun's vast orb,
Source of light, life, and joy, the glittering worlds
That now ‘resound with mirth,’[1] shall all be quench'd
And blotted in the gloom of ancient night,
Which in the day of wrath shall come again.
But Thought can never die ! The gentle prayer
Of childhood's lisping lips shall rise beyond
The murky clouds, and find a welcome full
At God's right hand, for ever in His breast,
Who on the earth was once a little child.
The deep, foul whisper of the murderer hoarse
Shall cleave the midnight air, and echo wide
Through time and space. Whisper and prayer alike
Shall then come forth, when He shall speak who cried,
‘ Ephphătha,’[2] ‘ Be openĕd :’ and deeply sigh'd,
Foreseeing many should abuse that gift.
Yea, He will take account, in that dread day,
Of every word that now men idly speak.[3]

---

[1] Wordsworth's *Peter Bell.*
[2] Mark vii. 24.   [3] Matthew xii. 36.

Deem it not strange, O unbelieving heart !
That this should be ; for God, who fashion'd us,
Hath,' in His wisdom, placed within our breasts,
A faithful witness of our inmost thoughts.
He seems to slumber oft ; our busy hearts
Heed him not now ; but at th' appointed hour,
In accents clear and thrilling, shall he tell
Each thought, and word, and deed forgotten long,
And bid them pass before the soul's sear'd sight.

A sage[1] has told of one, a humble maid,
Who,·in the deep seclusion of a vale,
'Midst the Swiss mountains, with a pastor dwelt,
A studious man, who oft his garden paced
And spent a vacant hour, speaking aloud
To his own raptured ear, the words of men
Of old renown'd, and in their native tongues—
The Hebrew Psalmist, and the sightless Bard
Who tells of Troy, and man's short life compares
To falling leaves,[2] or speaks of shepherd's joys,
While gazing calmly on the distant hills
And silent woods, beneath the moon's soft light.[3]

Now, it should seem, these oft-repeated strains
Had gently glided through the maiden's ear,
Who plied her needle at a casement by,
And, all to her unknown, had found a place

[1] Coleridge, in *The Friend.*
[2] *Iliad* VI. 146.   [3] *Iliad* VIII. 551.

Deep in her inner self.   Sounds strange and mean-
      ingless
To her they were : but in her heart were bound
By some mysterious link, which Nature forged.
Years after, she fell sick of fever ; and, at times,
When the worst stage was on her, she would speak
Words from the Psalms, and from the tale of Troy,
With all preciseness, which, by some who knew,
Were recognised for those the pastor spake
Oft, as he daily paced his garden-walk.
God bless'd the means of cure ; the maid was well :
But, in her health, the words she often spake
In sickness, strange to tell ! she had forgotten quite :
Nor did she seem to know those once familiar
      sounds.

'Tis this same power which often summons forth,
From the dark treasury of former years,
Things long-forgotten.   Oft the spicy breeze
Wafted from Taprobana's Isle[1] has brought
To the rude pirate's heart, a crushing sense
Of violence and lawless deeds, till then
Forgotten.   Oft the yellow gorse-bud's scent
Hath made the dweller in some dingy lane
Hot tears of penitence to shed, and mourn
The happy days, when o'er the broomy hills
Or sea-wash'd cliffs, in innocence she roam'd.

[1] Ceylon.

Oh! pause and ponder well thy wondrous frame,
Vain, thoughtless man! Whence camest thou, O
    think ?
And whither tendest ? What thou doest here,
Ay, or what thinkest, ne'er shalt thou forget.
Let but the key-note sound, at God's command,
And, straightway, deep vibrations echo forth
Things long-forgotten. In that dreadful day,
When the last trumpet's wondrous note shall sound,[1]
Rending the spheres, and piercing the dull tomb,
The wheel of each man's destiny shall roll
Backwards,. unfolding all his inner life ;
From his last breath to childhood's earliest sin,
Which led him first from God, all shall be told.
Some, too, who in the world's esteem were great,
Cæsars and Pontiffs, then shall sudden start
(Their thoughts unfolded to their guilty sight)
From the fond dream of pride ; and deep dismay
And "everlasting shame "[2] their hearts shall freeze.
Where shall *we* find a refuge in that day ?
In Him alone, whose spotless robe can hide
The sins of those who seek Him here on earth,
Ere yet the tomb be closed that shuts us in.

    Kirkside, *February* 22, 1854.

        [1] Mira spargit tuba sonum
          Par sepulchra regionum.— *The Sequence.*
       [2] Dan. xii. 2.

On a Snowy, Sunshine Day.

SEE the snow-flake's frequent flowing
  Down the calm and silent sky,
Through the lift so blue and glowing,
  Resting-place for prayer's meek eye.

See yon sun, who ne'er is weary
  Shedding down his golden light :
Even winter sad and dreary,
  Thinks not now of chilly night.

Many a slender spray is bending
  'Neath a load of feath'ry flakes ;
Though it felt them not descending,
  Yet at length it bends and breaks.

Here for ever could I linger
  Gazing on a sight so fair,
Traced by God's unerring finger
  On this hill-top bleak and bare.

Soon high clouds are fiercely riding
  O'er the sky that late was still ;
Now his face bright Sol is hiding,
  And the blast moans round the hill.

All things drooping seem to sorrow,
    And to dread some coming ill ;
They forget that on the morrow
    All may yet be bright and still.

Now the branches too are swinging
    To the surly moaning blast,
Now I see them upward springing
    From their load relieved at last.

As the glistering, melting treasure
    Bends to earth the loaded spray ;
So false dreams of youthful pleasure
    Bind us to our mother clay.

Oft the traveller, delighted,
    Pauses 'midst the Alpine snows,
Gazing, and at length benighted,
    Yields to Death in soft repose.

But when biting winds are blowing,
    Closely wrapt, with earnest soul,
He, all else around unknowing,
    Onward presses to the goal.

Thus we dream ; some golden morrow
    Here on earth still hope to see,
Till the timely voice of sorrow
    Bid the fair illusion flee.

Oft afflicted do we murmur,
  Nor the fiend that wounds us know ;
But at last, when faith grows firmer,
  We shall bless the day of woe.

When grief comes, O rashly deem not
  That our Father is unkind ;
As they are, in dreams, things seem not :
  Hearts asleep, like eyes, are blind.

Can I doubt that God is holy,
  Full of love and full of truth,
Guiding us by lessons slowly
  Through the mazy paths of youth !

Yes ! above, below, around us,
  Forward on our homeward way ;
From the death-like sleep around us,
  All things beckon us away.

As we float adown the river
  Of a bright and golden youth,
Let us deem that it may bear us
  To a sea of endless ruth.

But when sorrows round us gather
  As we wayward daily roam,
They're but voices from our Father
  Sent to call us to our home.

Upward through the cloud-land rifted
  Of dull earth, my spirit rise,
By pure faith and hope uplifted
  To Thy home beyond the skies !

KIRKSIDE, 1854.

On the Disappearance of the Snow, and the Sight of the First Snow-drop at Kirkside.— March 1, 1855.

'LOCKED in ice the sounding river, bound in frost the earth hath been,
Snow-clad lawn and feather'd branches through the moonlight soft are seen ;
Fair the sight, but quickly fading as the hopes which maidens dream :
Cold and cheerless as the pleasures of this life to old men seem.'

So we mused, and thankful laid us down to ' take the gift of sleep'[1]
(Many weary hearts are breaking, many waking eyes now weep) ;
Soon we hear the mighty cadence of the blast that sweeps along—
Not the moan of surly winter—'tis beneficent as strong.

Rude its voice, yet somewhat kindly does it burst upon my ear,
Straightway green fields, buds, and blossoms to my fancy's eye appear ;

[1] ὕπνου δῶρον ἕλοντο. —*Iliad* VII. 484.

All things by God's hand are temper'd, and a holy
    end fulfil ;
Troubles cast the shades which give us ' resting-places
    calm and still.'[1]

Rightly had I deem'd ; at morning, when I went to
    meet the sun,
On the slopes the green earth saw I, for the snow
    was past and gone.
From the glowing south the tempest, over Afric's
    burning sands,
Thirsty came and drank the ice-cold fountains of the
    snowy lands.

Now I heard the birds rejoicing in the soft returning
    spring ;
Full of pleasure were their motions as they spread
    the glitt'ring wing :
While I gaze I spied a snow-drop's tiny bud just
    bursting through ;
It hath borne the winter's darkness with a spirit meek
    and true.

Biding still the time appointed, full of hope amid the
    gloom,
Now sublimed, and pure, and spotless, see it spring-
    ing from the tomb !
Such is many a gentle spirit, taught in youth the yoke
    to bear,
Rising up through boyhood's troubles to a manhood
    strong and fair !

[1] Wordsworth's ' Song for the Wandering Jew.'

Such are they who, patient waiting through the long
   and troubled night,
Upward spring to meet the Day-star in the upland
   fields of light !
Oft their faith and hope are failing as they journey
   here below,
But at length they rise triumphant over sin, and
   death, and woe.

Whispers from above are calling in each breeze that
   fans the spray ;
Waving boughs and clouds uprising seem to beckon
   us away :
Thus our hearts, long unobservant, satisfied on earth
   to roam,
Oft may hear from things around us gentle calls to
   ' fetch us home.'[1]

     [1] Collect for Good Friday.

KIRKSIDE, *March* 1, 1855.

To my Godchild, Ellen Dudding,
on her first Birthday.

THROUGH a year of days, the earth,
  Circling round the sun, has pass'd :
Millions full of woe or mirth
  Bearing on her bounteous breast.

One there is, a yearling mild,
  This day twelvemonths past, that came
To this world rough and wild—
  Ellen is her gentle name.

Passing through this desert bare,
  As a child of grace to heav'n,
Pledged her Saviour's cross to bear,
  She to God was duly giv'n.

Kindly thoughts, at eve, of thee,
  Oft, my godchild dear, have I ;
Oft my humble prayers for thee,
  Rise up through the morning sky.

Through a childhood soft and fair,
  Through a bright and glowing youth,

May thy soul Christ's likeness wear,
  Full of gentleness and truth.

Be in womanhood's full stage
  Thy father's pride, thy mother's friend :
Kind and cheerful be thine age,
  Calm and full of hope thine end !

KIRKSIDE, *April* 2, 1855.

On the Falling Leaf.

JUST as the falling leaf is man !
   His days are but a summer's span.
Down he drops ; and o'er him sighs
The wintry wind, and off he flies,
Through the grey and gusty air,
Through gloom and darkness—where ! oh where !
Vanish'd in the closing night,
Shall he ne'er again see light ?
Yes ! that feeble, falt'ring soul,
Long tempest-toss'd from pole to pole,
When ages long have pass'd away,
And brought the burning Judgment Day,
When the last trumpet's wondrous sound
Awakes the nations under ground,
Rénds the rocks, and cleaves the air.
Yes ! that trembling soul is there.
Went it forth in doubt and gloom
To the dark and narrow tomb ?
Yes ! but one drop of blood was spilt,
To cleanse its deep despairing guilt !
Trusting, it saw, and breathed the prayer
Of weakest faith, next to despair :
Then rising past the dying throes
Of earth, and ocean, and the woes

Of waning suns, 'twill pierce the dome
Of heav'n, and reach its endless home.
O wondrous love! lowly and meek
And patient!   All who JESUS seek
Shall find Him knocking at the door
Of yielding hearts, though hard before!

KIRKSIDE. *Aug.* 18, 1856.

Words for Keble's Air.

SOFTLY the daylight has faded away,
  Gone are the bright golden glories of day,
    Chilly around us drops the night ;
Lead us, O Father, and lend us Thy light.

Dark is all nature ; but darker the soul :
Give us Thy Spirit to guide and control
    From risks and dangers of this night ;
Guard us, O Father, and lend us Thy light.

Soon shall the troubles of this life be past :
Better and brighter hopes let us hold fast,
    Till all the clouds of sin's dark night
Melt in the dawn of the Advent's great light.

Jesus ! our Saviour, Redeemer, and King,
Nightly Thy praise would we joyfully sing,
    Hail Thee each dawn, till Advent's light
Burst on our spirits resurgent and bright !

PORTOBELLO, *Septr.* 29, 1858.

Air—' Tantum Ergo Sacramentum.'

SEE the golden dawn arise !
　　Lord, it comes from Thee !
Blessed light now cheers our eyes,
　　And Thy love we see.
May Thy light reviving,
Through the deep gloom striving,
Cheer our hearts and guide us ever,
Till we reach that haven blest
　　　Of eternal rest !

Through the dark and stormy night
　　Of life's troubled sea,
To the land of peace and light
　　We are led by Thee ;
May Thy Spirit guide us,
And, whate'er betide us,
Health or sickness, joy or sorrow,
Let us wait the dawning ray
　　　Of Thy coming day !

Faithless hearts the Lord forsake :
　　Oft they doubt His truth ;
Wandering bypaths oft they take—
　　Paths to shame and ruth.

Let a joyous morrow
Break their night of sorrow,
Cheer their souls, and steadfast ever
Keep them in the troubled way,
Ending in bright day!

Hearts that simple are and pure
In Thy love rejoice :
Ever steadfast, ever sure,
Listening to Thy voice—
Ever keep us, Jesus,
From our sins release us,
Bear our burdens, and rejoicing,
Keep us by thy helping power
Till Thine advent hour!

NORTH BERWICK, *Aug.* 1860.

Dr. Theophilus Thompson, who died August 14, 1860.

O DEAR Theophilus! my early friend !
　　Oft, as in youth, I marked the holy aim
That guided thee, through life, to its blest end,
My heart was cleansed.   Before the lark's first flight,
We clomb the mountains oft ; and converse sweet.
Of holy hopes and aspirations bright
Were wont to hold, such as for youth is meet.
And oft the strains of the old English muse.
By each repeated, soothed the listening ear :
Words, too, of Southey and the great Recluse
Of Rydal, both to each of us so dear.
Such was thy youth! Thy manhood wise was given,
Like Christ's, to healing arts, and leading souls to
　　heav'n !

TYNINGHAME WOODS, HADDINGTONSHIRE,
　　　　Aug. 18, 1860.

Translation from Lucretius.

Lib. II. 14.

O MISERAS hominum mentes ! O pectora cæca !
Qualibus in tenebris vitæ, quantisque periclis
Degitur hoc ævi, quodcumque 'st ! Nonne videre
Nil aliud sibi Naturam latrare, nisi ut, cum
Corpore sejunctus dolor absit, mente fruatur
Jucundo sensu, curâ semotâ, metuque !

TRANSLATION.

' O wretched minds of men ! O blinded breasts !
' In how deep darkness, far from life and light,
' In how great perils, passes this sad life !
' Whate'er, where'er it be ! Is it not but to see
' That for nought else does helpless Nature yell
' But for that day, when, from this flesh escaped,
' We shall be free from pain, and shall drink in
' A flood of joy, when care and grief are past !'

So mourn'd a poet, who in darkness dwelt,
And knew not Christ, the Life, the Light, the Way.
Oh, if he saw the baseness of this life,
Its poor unmeetness for our higher hopes,
Shall *we*, who know Christ's love, choose for our
home
This fleeting world, and so neglect to seek,
Through His good Spirit, our eternal rest ?

PORTLAND RECTORY,
January 1861.

Translation from Lucretius.

Lib. II. I.

SUAVE, mari magno turbantibus æquora ventis,
 E terra magnum alterius spectare laborem :
Non quia vexari quemquam 'st jucunda voluptas,
Sed quibus ipse malis careas, quia cernere suave 'st.

TRANSLATIONS. -

'Tis sweet, when angry surges fiercely roar,
And the proud billows thunder on the shore,
Amidst the foaming surf some hapless bark,
Whilst we on shore are safe, toiling to mark ;
Not that we love our fellows' woes to see,
But still 'tis sweet to note what risks we flee !

ANOTHER.

'Tis sweet, whilst far at sea the bounding billows roar,
And the hoarse surges thunder on the sounding shore.
Safely, from some fair mead, with anxious eye, to mark,
Amidst the angry surf, a peril-stricken bark ;
Not that my heart delights my fellows' woes to see,
But yet 'tis sweet to see the ills from which we're free !

ANOTHER.

'Tis sweet, whilst far away at sea, the angry surges
  hoarsely roar,
And the proud billows in their rage burst fiercely on
  the sounding shore,

Amidst the raging surf, that boiling foams, a peril-
stricken bark,

Safe and at rest, from some green mead, with anxious
eye, safely to mark ;

Not that I would, with heartless breast, the sufferings
of my fellows see ;

But 'tis yet sweet, in peace to see those ills from which
ourselves are free.

PORTLAND RECTORY,
March 28, 1861.

Translation from Homer.

ILIAD VI. 146.

Οἵη περ φύλλων γενεὴ, τοίηδε καὶ ἀνδρῶν.
Φύλλα τὰ μέν τ' ἄνεμος χαμάδις χέει, ἄλλα δέ θ' ὕλη
Τηλεθόωσα φύει, ἔαρος δ' ἐπιγίγνεται ὥρη·
Ὡς ἀνδρῶν γενεὴ, ἡ μὲν φύει, ἡ δ' ἀπολήγει

TRANSLATION.

Dear fellow-traveller, pause awhile to see
　　Yon Autumn tree !
The winds bear down to earth the dry, sere leaves :
　　My heart perceives
An emblem there of our poor mortal race
Who live to fall, and the green earth deface !

But, when the Spring's reviving power is seen,
　　The leaves are green ;
The old are gone, a new and joyous race
　　Then takes their place.
'Tis thus with man !　The father's in the grave :
The boy the bright earth walks, in joy right brave.

PORTLAND RECTORY,
　　March 16, 1861.

Translation from Homer.

ILIAD VIII 555.

'Ὡς δ' ὅτ' ἐν οὐρανῷ ἄστρα φαεινὴν ἀμφὶ σελήνην
Φαίνετ' ἀριπρεπέα, ὅτε τ' ἔπλετο νήνεμος αἰθήρ,
"Ἐκ τ' ἔφανον πᾶσαι σκοπιαί, καὶ πρώονες ἄκροι
Καὶ νάπαι οὐρανόθεν δ' ἄρ' ὑπερράγη ἄσπετος αἰθήρ,
Πάντα δέ τ' εἴδεται ἄστρα· γέγηθε δέ τε φρένα ποιμήν.

TRANSLATION.

When in the Heavens, around the beaming moon,
The stars, in wondrous brightness, circling roll,
In the deep stillness of the evening hour,
When every mountain-top is bathed in light,
And the high forelands and the wooded dells,
Through rifted veil of boundless ether, clear
And sharp are seen, and we may view all round
The countless stars : 'tis then, indeed, the swain,
On the smooth uplands, 'midst the glorious light,
Tending his flock, drinks gladness to his breast.

PORTLAND RECTORY,
March 16, 1861.

To Eliza.

DEAR, gentle child ! a mother's care,
　Silent, devout, sincere,
Hail'd every grace of form and heart
　That mark'd each passing year.

God call'd her calm, meek spirit home
　To her appointed rest ;
Beneath the grassy sod she waits
　A resurrection blest.

Yet thou art not left desolate
　To wander on the earth :
Her spirit tends thy summer walks,
　And hallows all thy mirth.

She pities all thy childish fears :
　Through winter's whirling snows,
Unseen, she guides thee ; and around
　Mysterious shelter throws.

Dear Margaret watches thee on earth :
　And in her full, mild eyes　　·
Thy mother's love reflected, thou
　Mayst see with fond surprise.

To Eliza.

Oft have *I* seen, to *her* unknown,
  A sister's love give place
To deeper thoughts of tenderness,
  While gazing on thy face.

And I have mark'd her parting kiss,
  And caught her soft ' Good night,'
As she squeezed thy little hand in hers,
  With a mother's full delight.

Nor have I seen with heart untouch'd
  Dear Dora's buoyant mirth,
Swinging thy hand in hers, she goes.
  Euphrosyne,[1] by birth.

And there are those who love thee well,
  Far o'er the distant sea ;
And on each breeze they ' send a thought
  And a wish after thee.'[2]

Dear child ! go on thy way—thrice blest.
  In *her* that went before,
In those that God has given thee now,
  In friends He has in store.

June 10, 1844.

[1] The Goddess of Joy.   [2] Cowper.

H

APPENDIX.

APPENDIX

Containing some Extracts from Orthodox Fathers as to Valentinianism.

I ADD some extracts from the orthodox Fathers, as to the great heresy of Valentinianism and its evil tendency, for the information of those who feel an interest in the subject. I content myself by citing some passages from Irenæus, A.D. 167 ; Tertullianus, A.D. 192 ; Clemens Alexandrinus, A.D. 192 : and Augustinus Hipponensis, A.D. 396.

The first extract is from one of the Greek fragments in the Paris edition of Irenæus, by Feuardentius, who added many commentaries. It is at Lib. I. cap. vi. of *Irenæi, Contra Hæreses :*—ὡς μηδὲ τῆς παρὰ Θεῷ καὶ ἀνθρώποις μεμισημένης τῆς τῶν θηριομάχων καὶ μονομαχίας ἀνδροφόνου θέας ἀπέχεσθαι ἐνίους αὐτῶν. οἱ δὲ καὶ ταῖς τῆς σαρκὸς ἡδοναῖς κατακόρως δουλεύοντες, τὰ σαρκικὰ τοῖς σαρκικοῖς, καὶ τὰ πνευματικὰ τοῖς πνευματικοῖς ἀποδίδοσθαι λέγουσι. καὶ οἱ μὲν αὐτῶν λάθρα τὰς διδασκομένας ὑπ' αὐτῶν τὴν διδαχὴν ταύτην γυναῖκας διαφθείρουσιν, ὡς πολλάκις ὑπ' ἐνίων αὐτῶν ἐξαπατηθεῖσαι, ἔπειτα ἐπιστρέψασαι γυναῖκες εἰς τὴν ἐκκλησίαν τοῦ Θεοῦ, σὺν τῇ λοιπῇ πλάνῃ καὶ τοῦτο ἐξωμολογήσαντο· οἱ δὲ καὶ κατὰ τὸ

φανερὸν ἀπερυθριάσαντες ὧν ἂν ἐρασθῶσι γυναικῶν.
ταύτας ἀπ᾽ ἀνδρῶν ἀποσπάσαντες. ἰδίως γαμετὰς ἡγή-
σαντο. ἄλλοι δὲ αὖ πάλιν σεμνῶς κατ᾽ ἀρχὰς. ὡς μετὰ
ἀδελφῶν προσποιούμενοι συνοικεῖν, προϊόντος τοῦ χρόνου
ἠλέγχθησαν, ἐγκύμονος τῆς ἀδελφῆς ὑπὸ τοῦ ἀδελφοῦ
γενηθείσης.

Καὶ ἄλλα δὲ πολλὰ μυσαρὰ καὶ ἄθεα πράσσοντες.
ἡμῶν μὲν διὰ τοῦ φόβου τοῦ Θεοῦ φυλασσομένων καὶ
μέχρις ἐννοίας καὶ λόγου ἁμαρτεῖν, κατατρέχουσιν, ὡς
ἰδιωτῶν, καὶ μηδὲν ἐπισταμένων· ἑαυτοὺς δὲ ὑπερυψοῦσι.
τελείους ἀποκαλοῦντες καὶ σπέρματα ἐκλογῆς.

The next consists of scattered passages of Tertullian, from his book *Adversus Valentinianos.* His
style is wordy and crabbed, and he speaks very
strongly against those heretics :—' Nihil magis
curant quàm occultare quod prædicant ; si tamen
prædicant qui occultant. Custodiæ officium, con-
scientiæ officium est. Confusio prædicatur, dum
religio adseveratur.' Again : · Pudiciores alii, hono-
rem Divinitatis recordati, ut etiam unius conjugii
dedecus ab eo avellerent, maluerunt nullum Bytho
sexum deputare ; et fortasse Hoc Deum, non Hic
Deus, neutro genere pronunciant. Alii contra magis
et masculum et fœminam dicunt, ne apud solos
Lunenses Hermaphroditum existimet, annalium
commentator Fenestella.' Then again : ' De ipso
jam Domino Jesu, quanta diversitas scinditur ? Hi
ex omnium *æonum* flosculis eum construunt, illi ex
solis decem constitisse contendunt, quos Sermo et
vita protulerunt. Inde et in ipsum Sermonis et Vitæ

concurrerunt oculi. Isti ex duodecim potius, ex Homi
nibus et Ecclesiæ fœtu; ideóque filium hominis aiunt
pronunciatum : alii a Christo et Spiritu Sancto constabi-
liendæ universitati provisis, confictum : et jure, paternæ
appellationis hæredem. Sunt qui filium hominis
aliunde conceperint dicendum ; quamquam ipsum
Patrem pro magno nominis sacramento Hominem
appellasse presumpserint, ut quid amplius speres de
ejus Dei fide cui nunc adæquaris ? Talia ingenia
superfruticant apud illos ex materni seminis redun
dantiâ. Atque ita inolescentes doctrinæ Valentinianorum, in sylvas jam exoleverunt Gnosticorum.'

Next I cite a passage of Clemens Alexandrinus from
his *Stromatum* Lib. VII. p. 349 :—οἱ τὰς αἱρέσεις
ἐπαινοήσαντες γεγόνασι, καὶ μέχρι γε τῆς 'Αντωνίνου
τοῦ πρεσβυτέρου διέτειναν ἡλικίας, καθάπερ ὁ Βασι-
λείδης, κἂν Γλαυκίαν ἐπιγράφηται διδάσκαλον, ὡς
αὐχοῦσιν αὐτοὶ, τὸν Πέτρου ἑρμηνέα. ὡς αὕτως δὲ
καὶ Οὐαλεντῖνον Θεοδάδι ἀκηκοέναι φέρουσιν· γνώριμος
δ' οὗτος ἐγεγόνει Παύλου,—thus trying to prove his
respectability by his pretended friendship with an
associate of Paul. (For these views on marriage,
and their gross indelicacy, see the *Stromata*, pp. 311
and 319 of the Leyden folio edition, 1616, by Daniel
Heinsius.)

Last, I take Augustine's book, *De Hæresibus :—*
' Valentiniani à Valentino, qui de natura rerum
multa fabulosa confinxit : Triginta αἰῶνας, *id est*, secula
asserens extitisse, quorum principium esse profundum
et silentium, quod profundum etiam patrem appellat.

Ex quibus duobus velut conjugio processisse per-
hibet intellectum et veritatem, et protulisse in hono-
rem patris *æonas* octo. De intellectu, autem, et veri-
tate processisse verbum et vitam et protulisse æonas
decem. Porro de verbo et vita processisse Hominem
et Ecclesiam et protulisse *æonas* duodecim. Itaque
octo et decem et duodecim fieri Triginta *æonas*, ha-
bentes, ut diximus, primum principium de profundo
et silentio. Christum, autem a Patre missum, id est,
a profundo spiritale vel cœleste corpus secum attu-
lisse : nihilque assumpsisse de Virgine Maria sed per
illam, tanquam per rimam, aut per fistulam, sine
ullâ de illâ assumptâ carne, transisse. Dé tricesimo
sæculo, dicit, Diabolum genitum et a Diabolo alios
natos qui fecerint hunc mundum. Et ideó malitiam
non arbitrio tribuit, sed naturæ mundi, *id est*, generi
diabolico carnis resurrectionem negat, animam tantum
et spiritum affirmat per Christum salvari. *Secundiani*,
hoc a *Valentinianis* distare dicuntur, quod addunt
opera turpitudinis. Ptolemæus, quoque discipulus
Valentini, hæresim novam condere cupiens, quatuor
æonas et alias quatuor asserere maluit."

I at first looked into the *Commonitorium* of *Vin-
centius Lirinensis*, A.D. 494, where I never doubted I
should find a brief view of the errors of *Valentine*.
To my surprise, the subject is quite unnoticed by
him ; and this is explained by the fact that the author
had himself a strong leaning to that heresy.

EDINBURGH : T. CONSTABLE PRINTER TO HER MAJESTY

www.ingramcontent.com/pod-product-compliance
Lightning Source LLC
Chambersburg PA
CBHW020407030726
47496CB00007B/2337